Assessing Aid

A World Bank Policy Research Report

Assessing Aid

What Works, What Doesn't, and Why

Published for the World Bank
OXFORD UNIVERSITY PRESS

Oxford University Press

OXFORD   NEW YORK   TORONTO
DELHI   BOMBAY CALCUTTA   MADRAS   KARACHI
KUALA LUMPUR   SINGAPORE   HONG KONG   TOKYO
NAIROBI   DAR ES SALAAM   CAPE TOWN
MELBOURNE   AUCKLAND

and associated companies in

BERLIN   IBADAN

*© 1998 The International Bank for Reconstruction
and Development / The World Bank
1818 H Street, N.W.
Washington, D.C. 20433*

*Published by Oxford University Press, Inc.
200 Madison Avenue, New York, N.Y. 10016*

*Manufactured in the United States of America
First printing November 1998
Third printing October 1999*

*The boundaries, colors, denominations, and other information shown on the maps in this vol-
ume do not imply on the part of the World Bank Group any judgment on the legal status of
any territory or the endorsement or acceptance of such boundaries.*

Library of Congress Cataloging-in-Publication (CIP) Data.

*Assessing aid : what works, what doesn't, and why.
    p. cm -- (A World Bank policy research report)
  "Published for the World Bank."
  Includes bibliographical references.
  ISBN 0-19-521123-5
  1. Economic assistance. 2. Economic assistance--Evaluation. I.
World Bank. II. Series.
  HC60 .A836 1998
  338.9--ddc21*

                                   *98-33286
                                      CIP*

∞ *Text printed on paper that conforms to the American National Standard
for Permanence of Paper for Printed Library Materials, Z39.48-1984*

Contents

Foreword

FOREIGN AID IS AS MUCH ABOUT KNOWLEDGE AS IT IS ABOUT MONEY. Helping countries and communities generate the knowledge that they need for development is a prime role of assistance. And aid itself is a learning business that continually evolves as lessons of success and failure become clear.

Assessing Aid is a contribution to this ongoing learning process. It aims to contribute to a larger "rethinking of aid" that the international community is engaged in—a rethinking in two senses. First, with the end of the cold war, there is a group that is "rethinking aid" in the sense of questioning its very existence in a world of integrated capital markets. In response to this trend, we show that there remains a role for financial transfers from rich countries to poor ones.

Second, developing and developed nations alike are reconceptualizing the role of assistance in light of a new development paradigm. Effective aid supports institutional development and policy reforms that are at the heart of successful development. Though tremendous progress has been made in the past 50 years, global poverty remains a severe problem.

Research into aid, growth, and poverty reduction provides important evidence about making aid more effective. This report summarizes the findings of recent World Bank research on aid effectiveness. The primary research has been published or will soon be published in professional journals. This report aims to disseminate the findings to a broad audience. It should be stressed that there are important aspects of development cooperation that have not been covered by the research. The report restricts itself to areas where we have new findings.

Aid is channeled through a variety of activities that bring a mix of money and ideas. Two key themes emerge in this report. One theme is that effective aid requires the right timing and the second that it requires the right mix of money and ideas.

The timing of assistance is crucial in helping countries improve their policies and institutions. When countries reform their economic policies, well-timed assistance can increase the benefits of reform and maintain popular support for them. Similarly, at the local level, when communities organize themselves to improve services, the availability of aid can make the difference between successful innovation and failure.

On the mix of activities, we find that money has a large impact—but only in low-income countries with sound management. Before countries reform, finance has little impact. Thus, donors need to rely on other instruments to support development in the distorted environments—and the report looks in detail at what is likely to work and what, not.

To have a greater effect on global poverty reduction through equitable and sustainable development, foreign assistance requires a three-way partnership among recipient countries, aid agencies, and donor countries.

The recipient countries must be moving towards sound policies and institutions. The active involvement of civil society can help sustain this sound management in developing countries. The good news here is that many poor countries have initiated serious reforms in policies and governance, so that the climate for effective aid is the best that it has been in decades.

Development agencies must shift away from total disbursements and the narrow evaluation of the physical implementation of projects to create high impact assistance. Agencies should be evaluated on the extent to which they have allocated their resources, both of finance and knowledge, to stimulate the policy reforms and institutional changes that improve people's lives. The good news here is that both bilateral and multilateral agencies are transforming themselves and cooperating together to become more effective.

Finally, citizens of donor countries must continue to support aid. The bad news is that just as aid is poised to be its most effective, the volume of aid is declining and is at its lowest level ever. This report is also aimed at persuading developed countries to continue to give aid and to take an active interest in development and development cooperation.

More effective development means improvements in the lives of hundreds of millions of people: more food on the table, healthier babies, more children in school. These are things worth fighting for—and properly managed, foreign aid can make a big contribution.

Joseph E. Stiglitz
Senior Vice-President for
    Development Economics and
    Chief Economist
The World Bank
November 1998

The Report Team

THIS POLICY RESEARCH REPORT WAS WRITTEN BY DAVID DOLLAR and Lant Pritchett of the Development Research Group. It culminates a research program on aid effectiveness initiated and supervised by Lyn Squire. Original research as background for this report includes work by the authors and by Craig Burnside, Klaus Deininger, Shanta Devarajan, William Easterly, Deon Filmer, Jonathan Isham, Dani Kaufmann, Elizabeth King, Jennie Litvack, Luis Serven, Lyn Squire, Vinaya Swaroop, and Jakob Svensson. The authors draw extensively on evaluations and studies done in other parts of the World Bank, which are cited throughout the text. Much of the underlying research was presented and discussed at the joint OECF-World Bank symposium, "A New Vision of Development Cooperation for the 21st Century" (Tokyo, September 1997). The authors would like to acknowledge excellent research assistance from Mita Chakraborty, Charles Chang, Giuseppe Iarossi, and Pablo Zoido-Lobaton and superb administrative support from Emily Khine, Kari Labrie, and Raquel Luz. Lawrence MacDonald provided helpful support throughout the preparation of the report. Bruce Ross-Larson, with Jessica Moore and Sharifah Albukhary, edited the report for publication.

The judgments in this policy research report do not necessarily reflect the views of the World Bank's Board of Directors or the governments they represent.

Rethinking the Money and Ideas of Aid

FOREIGN AID HAS AT TIMES BEEN A SPECTACULAR SUCCESS. Botswana and the Republic of Korea in the 1960s, Indonesia in the 1970s, Bolivia and Ghana in the late 1980s, and Uganda and Vietnam in the 1990s are all examples of countries that have gone from crisis to rapid development. Foreign aid played a significant role in each transformation, contributing ideas about development policy, training for public policymakers, and finance to support reform and an expansion of public services. Foreign aid has also transformed entire sectors. The agricultural innovations, investments, and policies that created the Green Revolution—improving the lives of millions of poor people around the world—were financed, supported, and disseminated through alliances of bilateral and multilateral donors. Internationally funded and coordinated programs have dramatically reduced such diseases as river blindness and vastly expanded immunization against key childhood diseases. Hundreds of millions of people have had their lives touched, if not transformed, by access to schools, clean water, sanitation, electric power, health clinics, roads, and irrigation—all financed by foreign aid.

On the flip side, foreign aid has also been, at times, an unmitigated failure. While the former Zaire's Mobuto Sese Seko was reportedly amassing one of the world's largest personal fortunes (invested, naturally, outside his own country), decades of large-scale foreign assistance left not a trace of progress. Zaire (now the Democratic Republic of Congo) is just one of several examples where a steady flow of aid ignored, if not encouraged, incompetence, corruption, and misguided polices. Consider Tanzania, where donors poured a colossal $2 billion into building roads over 20 years. Did the road network improve? No. For lack of maintenance, roads often deteriorated faster than they could be built.

Foreign aid has at times been a spectacular success—and an unmitigated failure.

Financial aid works in a good policy environment.

Foreign aid in different times and different places has thus been highly effective, totally ineffective, and everything in between. Perhaps that is to be expected in a complex endeavor that has spanned half a century, with scores of countries as donors, a hundred countries as recipients, tens of thousands of specific activities, and nearly $1 trillion in finance. But hindsight is valuable only if it produces insight. The checkered history of assistance has already led to improvements in foreign aid, and there is scope for further reform. The pressing question: How can development assistance be most effective at reducing global poverty?

The answer is needed urgently. While there has been more progress with poverty reduction in the past 50 years than in any comparable period in human history, poverty remains a dire global problem. More than a billion people live in extreme poverty—on less than $1 a day. Even more lack basic services that people in developed countries take for granted: clean water, sanitation, electricity, schooling. It is ironic—and tragic— that just as economic reform has created the best environment in decades for effective assistance, donors have cut aid back sharply. In 1997 OECD donors gave the smallest share of their GNPs in aid since comparable statistics began in the 1950s—less than one-quarter of 1 percent. It would take roughly a 50 percent increase even to restore aid to its 1991 level.

There have been many excellent studies of foreign aid.[1] But there are three important reasons to revisit this previously charted territory. First, recent shifts in the global economic and political environment—notably the end of the Cold War and the surge in private capital flows to the developing world—have affected the landscape for development assistance in a way that has left many questioning the very existence of aid. Second, there has been a shift in development strategy that requires a new approach to aid as a tactic within the evolving agenda. Third, there is new empirical evidence that provides insights into the puzzle of what is effective aid and what is ineffective aid.

This rethinking of aid produces the following findings:

■ *Financial aid works in a good policy environment.* Financial assistance leads to faster growth, poverty reduction, and gains in social indicators in developing countries with sound economic management. And the effect is large: with sound country management, 1 percent of GDP in assistance translates into a 1 percent decline in poverty and a similar decline in infant mortality. In a weak environment, however, money has much less impact. A $10 billion increase in aid would lift

25 million people a year out of poverty—but only if it favors countries with sound economic management. By contrast, an across-the-board increase of $10 billion would lift only 7 million people out of their hand-to-mouth existence.

- *Improvements in economic institutions and policies in the developing world are the key to a quantum leap in poverty reduction.* True, there have been sharp improvements in governance and policies in the past decade, but further reform of the same magnitude would lift another 60 million people a year out of poverty. When societies desire reform, foreign aid can provide critical support—in ideas, training, and finance. Efforts to "buy" policy improvements in countries where there is no movement for reform, by contrast, have typically failed.

- *Effective aid complements private investment.* In countries with sound economic management, foreign aid does not replace private initiative. Indeed, aid acts as a magnet and "crowds in" private investment by a ratio of almost $2 to every $1 of aid. In countries committed to reform, aid increases the confidence of the private sector and supports important public services. In highly distorted environments, aid "crowds out" private investment, which helps explain the small impact of aid in such cases.

- *The value of development projects is to strengthen institutions and policies so that services can be effectively delivered.* Aid brings a package of knowledge and finance. Most aid is delivered as investment projects in particular sectors such as roads, water supply, or education. Project finance, however, often does not increase spending in a sector any more than an untied grant would have—that is, aid finance is typically fungible. Thus, choosing such laudable sectors as primary health or education cannot ensure that money is well used. Aid is financing the entire public sector, and the overall quality of policies and institutions is the key to securing a large return from this finance. These findings highlight that the most critical contribution of projects is not to increase funding for particular sectors, but to help improve service delivery by strengthening sectoral and local institutions. The knowledge creation supported by aid leads to improvements in particular sectors, whereas the finance part of aid expands public services in general.

- *An active civil society improves public services.* One good idea that many projects have supported in recent years is a participatory approach to service delivery, often resulting in huge improvements. The best aid projects support initiatives that change the way the public sector does business.

The value of development projects is to strengthen institutions and policies so that services can be effectively delivered.

3

Financial assistance must be targeted more effectively to low-income countries with sound economic management.

The top-down, technocratic approach to project design and service delivery has not worked in areas critical for development—rural water supply, primary education, natural resource management, and many more.

■ *Aid can nurture reform in even the most distorted environments—but it requires patience and a focus on ideas, not money.* In some of the poorest countries of the world, the government is not providing effective policies or services, which is why government-to-government transfers have yielded poor results. Still, there are often champions of local or sectoral reform, and aid at times has been effective supporting these initiatives. This work is staff-intensive and results in little disbursement of funds. Successful assistance here aims to help reformers develop and test their ideas.

Making aid more effective in reducing poverty requires five policy reforms. First, financial assistance must be targeted more effectively to low-income countries with sound economic management. In a good policy environment financial assistance is a catalyst for faster growth, more rapid gains in social indicators, and higher private investment (chapter 1). In a poor policy environment, however, aid has much less impact. Clearly, poor countries with good policies should receive more financing than equally poor countries with weak economic management. Up until the early 1990s, however, finance has gone in equal amounts to well managed countries and to poorly managed ones. Furthermore, much of aid continues to go to middle-income countries that do not need it. It is possible to make aid more effectively targeted to poor countries and to better management simultaneously.

Second, policy-based aid should be provided to nurture policy reform in credible reformers. Experience shows that donor financing with strong conditionality but without strong domestic leadership and political support has generally failed to produce lasting change (chapter 2). Continued flows to governments that pay only lip service to reform have been a major problem. Policy-based financing should go only to countries with a strong track record or where there is a demonstrable basis for optimism (to support, for example, the concrete actions of domestically initiated reform efforts or a government newly chosen on a reform platform). New governments in post-conflict situations are often good candidates for support. In countries with poor policies and no credible reform movement, assistance should assume the more modest and patient role of disseminating ideas, transmitting experiences of other countries, training future policymakers and leaders, and stimulating capacity for informed policy debate within civil society. These measures are relatively inexpensive and do not conflict with the proposal that the bulk of finance should go to countries with sound economic management.

Third, the mix of aid activities should be tailored to country and sector conditions (chapter 3). Even where institutions and policies are weak, donors have tried to find something useful to finance. Surely it must be a good thing to finance primary health care or basic education? The evidence, however, is that aid is often fungible, so that what you see is not what you get. In circumstances where similar projects would have been undertaken anyway, donor money for particular projects and sectors does not necessarily "stick"—simply expands the government's budget. Thus even rigorous project selection or reallocation of donor finance to laudable activities cannot guarantee the effectiveness of aid in a distorted environment. To measure the effect of their finance, donors must look at overall allocations and, even more important, at the efficacy of public spending.

The allocation of expenditures alone does not guarantee success, for the quality of public spending is as important as its quantity. In countries with sound economic management (of both macroeconomic policy and delivery of public services), more aid can be in the form of budget support, which would simplify administration and reduce overhead. In countries with basically sound policies but weak capacity for delivering services, project aid should be a catalyst for improving the efficacy of public expenditures. Countries without good policies, efficient public services, or properly allocated expenditures will benefit little from financing, and aid should focus on improvements in all three areas.

Fourth, projects need to focus on creating and transmitting knowledge and capacity. The key role of development projects should be to support institutional and policy changes that improve public service delivery (chapter 4). Even where money may not stick, the local knowledge and institutional capacity created by the catalyst of aid projects can. Where projects are innovative, it is crucial to have objective and rigorous evaluation of outcomes and dissemination of new information. Knowledge about what works in service provision—and what does not—is one of the most important outputs of development assistance. In many cases innovative approaches to service delivery will involve greater participation by local communities and decentralization of decisionmaking.

Policy-based aid should be provided to nurture policy reform in credible reformers.

Aid agencies need to find alternative approaches to helping highly distorted countries, since traditional methods have failed.

Fifth, aid agencies need to find alternative approaches to helping highly distorted countries, since traditional methods have failed in these cases (chapter 5). Communities and governments are heterogeneous, and even in the most difficult environments there will be pockets of reform. Donors need to be patient and flexible and look for windows of opportunity to nurture these reform efforts. Typically, ideas will be more useful than large-scale finance. Donors' ability to work in these environments has been hampered by an "approval and disbursement culture" that does not value small-scale, staff-intensive activities. In the past agencies have too often focused on how much money they disburse and on narrow physical implementation measures of the "success" of the projects that they finance. It turns out that neither measure tells much about the effectiveness of assistance. The evaluation of development aid should focus instead on the extent to which financial resources have contributed to sound policy environments. It should focus on the extent to which agencies have used their resources to stimulate the policy reforms and institutional changes that lead to better outcomes. These are not easy questions to answer, but independent reviews of development agencies—with participation of developing country policymakers and project beneficiaries—can help establish whether agencies are doing a good job.

Box 1   Defining Aid

WHAT IS THE DIFFERENCE BETWEEN OFFICIAL development assistance and official development finance? The first is a subset of the second and comprises grants plus concessional loans that have at least a 25 percent grant component. Official development finance is all financing that flows from developed country governments and multilateral agencies to the developing world. Some of this financing is at interest rates close to commercial rates. "Foreign aid" is usually associated with official development assistance and normally targeted to the poorest countries. This assistance is the primary focus of this study, but many of the findings are relevant for the larger category of official development finance.

Both types of aid can be divided into bilateral and multilateral components. Bilateral assistance is adminis-

tered by agencies of donor governments (such as the U.S. Agency for International Development or Japan's Overseas Economic Cooperation Fund). Multilateral assistance is funded by contributions from wealthy countries and administered by agencies, such as the United Nations Development Programme and the World Bank. Of all official development assistance, roughly a third is multilateral.

Some bilateral aid is tied—that is, it must be used to procure goods and services from the donor country. Studies have shown that tied aid reduces the value of that assistance by about 25 percent, and there is widespread agreement that untying bilateral aid would make it more effective. Among OECD countries there has been a clear trend away from tied aid. In 1995 it accounted for only about a fifth of all aid.

The New International Environment

FOREIGN AID IS A POST WORLD WAR II PHENOMENON. FROM THE start, it had twin objectives, potentially in conflict. The first objective was to promote long-term growth and poverty reduction in developing countries; the underlying motivation of donors was a combination of altruism and a more self-interested concern that, in the long term, their economic and political security would benefit if poor countries were growing. The second objective was to promote the short-term political and strategic interests of donors. Aid went to regimes that were political allies of major Western powers. Thus the strategic and developmental objectives were potentially, but not necessarily, at odds. Consider Bolivia and Zaire. Both received U.S. aid, partly for strategic reasons, yet the outcomes were vastly different. Bolivia used the resources relatively well after reforms of the mid-1980s and over the past decade has stabilized and laid a groundwork for success. In the former Zaire, by contrast, it is hard to see any benefit from its years as a major aid recipient.

During the 1970s and 1980s foreign aid from OECD countries rose steadily (figure 1).[2] In 1991 official development assistance peaked at $69 billion (in 1995 prices; see boxes 1 and 2). In the 1990s, however, three events have lowered the absolute and relative importance of foreign aid: fiscal problems in OECD countries, the end of the Cold War, and the dramatic growth in private capital flows to developing countries.

In recent years OECD countries have been struggling to control fiscal deficits and contain growth in government spending. Even though foreign aid is a tiny fraction of budgets, it has been one of the first items for the ax. All major donors reduced aid relative to their GNPs between 1991 and 1997 (figure 2). The decline was especially sharp in the United States—aid was a mere 0.08 percent of GNP in 1997. Sweden and other Nordic countries have traditionally been generous, giving almost 1 percent of GNP. But among large countries, France is the only one that gives more than 0.45 percent. Collectively, OECD countries contributed just 0.22 percent of their GNP in 1997. The end of the Cold War likely influenced some countries' decisions. The strategic importance of aid has ebbed; as a result it risks losing its broad support among donor governments.

At the same time, there has been a surge in private capital flows to developing countries. In the 1970s and 1980s official finance—that is, money from bilateral donors and multilateral institutions—represented

After peaking in 1991, aid has fallen.

Figure 1 Financial Flows to Developing Countries

Billions of 1995 U.S. dollars

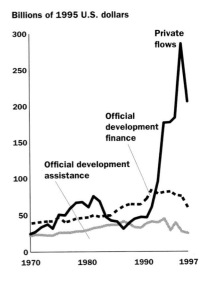

Source: Global Development Finance 1998.

7

Box 2 Measuring Aid

THE OECD'S DEVELOPMENT ASSISTANCE COMMITTEE publishes information on its members' aid to developing countries—that is, grants plus net disbursements of concessional loans that have at least a 25 percent grant component. A different way to measure aid is to extract from each concessional loan the grant element and add that to the figure for pure grants. Using this approach, Chang, Fernandez-Arias, and Serven (1998) developed data on aid for 103 recipients (see figure).

There are three points worth making about this new data. First, the adjusted figure tends to be lower than the traditional measure. Second, the two series are highly correlated and produce similar results in econometric analyses. Most aid is in the form of grants, so the new approach does not have much effect on the overall measure. The macroeconomic effects of aid are the same regardless of which measure of aid is used (see chapter 1). Third, the adjusted aid figures show a sharper decline in aid in the 1990s than the OECD measure. This is because international interest rates have been low in recent years, so the aid component of concessional loans is smaller. The amount of aid in a loan with a 2 percent interest rate is small if international interest rates are 5 percent and large if they are 10 percent.

Box figure 2 Total Aid: OECD Official Development Assistance and Adjusted Official Aid

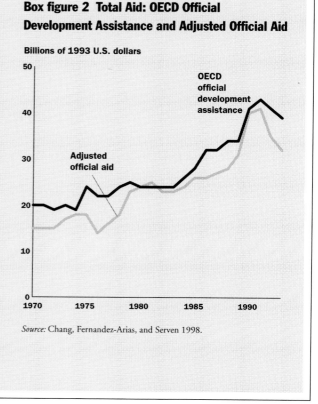

Billions of 1993 U.S. dollars

Source: Chang, Fernandez-Arias, and Serven 1998.

about half of all finance going from the developed to the developing world (see figure 1). With private flows expanding to more than $250 billion in 1996, however, official finance is now only a quarter of all finance available to developing countries.

Private capital flows are heavily concentrated in a few countries, however—and some flows are volatile. A surge in the late 1970s receded after the onset of the debt crisis in 1982. Another big rush occurred in the mid-1990s, but with the financial crises rocking East Asia in 1997 foreign investment dropped sharply. The flow of private money to the developing world fell by $80 billion between 1996 and 1997. In any event, private flows will continue to go to a small number of (mostly) middle-income countries. In 1996, 26 countries received 95 percent of private investment; the rest went to the other 140 developing countries.

Figure 2 Offical Development Assistance Relative to Gross National Product, Major Donors, 1991 and 1997

Aid is down everywhere.

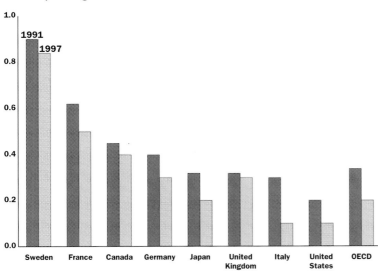

ODA as a percentage of GNP

Source: *World Development Indicators 1998.*

In a typical low-income country, foreign aid remains far and away the primary source of external finance, amounting to 7–8 percent of GNP.

Developments in the 1990s have sharply altered the climate for foreign aid. The end of the Cold War opened up new possibilities: with aid no longer constrained by those strategic objectives, it should be possible to make aid more efficient at meeting its primary objective of long-term growth and poverty reduction.[3] Yet, given budget problems and rising private flows, donors are clearly rethinking the importance and value of foreign assistance.

New Thinking on Development Strategy

FOREIGN AID, JUST ONE WAY OF PROMOTING DEVELOPMENT, MUST fit within a broad overall strategy. Past domestic and international political conditions and beliefs about development strategy structured organizations, instruments, and implementation of aid. But those beliefs have undergone enormous, and accelerating, change.

If all the aid to Zambia had gone into productive investment, it would be a rich country today.

Figure 3 The Gap between Model and Reality in Zambia, 1961–94

Thousands of 1995 U.S. dollars

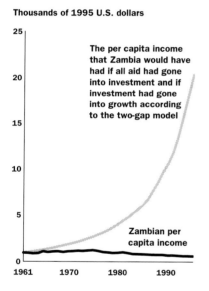

The per capita income that Zambia would have had if all aid had gone into investment and if investment had gone into growth according to the two-gap model

Zambian per capita income

Source: Easterly 1997.

In the early days of development assistance, government was seen as the positive agent for change. Domestic markets in developing countries were thought to be nonexistent and incapable of growth. International markets were tainted by the association with colonialism, as well as by the collapse of markets for commodities and credit in the Great Depression of the 1930s. In many developing countries the first flush of independence created optimism about new governments as agents of political, social, and economic change. Government-to-government aid had a plausible claim as the best way to promote development.

Development economists believed not only that poor countries were held back primarily by a lack of physical and human capital (which was, and remains, true) but also that domestic poverty and international market failures denied developing countries access to investment funds needed for economic growth.[4] Calculating countries' growth "requirements" of investment finance or foreign exchange (or both)—and comparing them with what was available—emphasized the size of the gaps to be filled. The natural tactical response was to fill the gaps with foreign aid through transfers of investible foreign exchange. If money was the problem, then "moving the money" was an appropriate objective for aid and aid agencies. The contribution of aid could then be measured in dollars.

Sadly, experience has long since undermined the rosy optimism of aid-financed, government-led, accumulationist strategies for development. Suppose that development aid only financed investment and investment really played the crucial role projected by early models. In that case, aid to Zambia should have financed rapid growth that would have pushed per capita income above $20,000, while in reality per capita income stagnated at around $600 (figure 3). The past 20 years have seen the death of centrally planned economies, stagnation in the leading import-substituting models of the 1970s (Mexico and Brazil), and broad economic failure (if not absolute disintegration) of post-independence Africa, which pursued a state-led strategy.[5] The past 20 years have also seen waves of spectacular increases in incomes and exports of East Asian economies—first, Korea, Taiwan (China), Hong Kong (now returned to China), and Singapore, followed by Thailand, Malaysia, Indonesia, and, after important economic reforms, China; the emergence of Chile as the most dynamic Latin American economy and the recent recovery of others; and successes in Africa, such as Botswana and Mauritius. The evidence suggests that rapid development is possible, and should be based on markets and on effective states playing an economically important facilitating, but not dominant, role.

So, there have been three phases of development thinking. In the first, market failures were seen as pervasive and complete, and government as the only solution to all ills. In the second there was a brief period when government failure was seen as pervasive and complete, and markets (if not the solution) as the only hope. Today's third view—pragmatic but not ideologically satisfying—is that both markets and governments have pervasive failures but that these usually are not complete. This emphasizes that government should focus on areas where the problems in the absence of intervention are greatest—but government must have the capacity to improve the situation. "We need to recognize both the limits and strengths of markets, as well as the strengths, and limits, of government interventions aimed at correcting market failures" (Stiglitz 1989, p. 202).

The development strategy emerging from this view is two-pronged—put in place growth-enhancing, market-oriented policies (stable macroeconomic environment, effective law and order, trade liberalization, and so on) and ensure the provision of important public services that cannot be well and equitably supplied by private markets (infrastructure services and education, for instance). Developing countries with sound policies and high-quality public institutions have grown much faster than those without—2.7 percent per capita compared with –0.5 percent per capita (box 3). Put simply, failures in policymaking, institution building, and the provision of public services have been more severe constraints on development than capital markets.

Together with the new strategy comes a broader agenda. Early development practice focused on growth of per capita income. But in reality, developing countries are concerned with broad improvements in the quality of life—higher incomes, yes, but also reduced poverty, advances in literacy and health, and environmentally sustainable development. The new agenda is reflected in the goals set forth by the donor community, in consultation with developing country partners:

- Reducing by one half the proportion of people living in extreme poverty by 2015.
- Achieving universal primary education in all countries by 2015.
- Making progress toward equality of the sexes and the empowerment of women by eliminating disparities in primary and secondary education by 2005.
- Reducing by two-thirds the mortality rates for infants and children under age 5 and by three-quarters maternal mortality—both by 2015.

Together with the new development strategy comes a broader agenda.

11

Box 3   Defining Sound Management: Good Policies and Institutions

SOUND MANAGEMENT CONSISTS OF THE INSTITUTIONS and policies that will lead to rapid development and poverty reduction in a particular country. Developing countries learn about good and bad policies from their own experience and each other's experience. Sound management is difficult but not impossible to measure using a number of proxy indicators.

Box figure 3 Institutions, Policies, and Growth

Annual percentage growth in real GDP per capita

Source: Burnside and Dollar 1998.

The index of economic policy used in box figure 3 combines three factors that have been shown in empirical studies to affect developing countries' growth: inflation, the budget surplus, and trade openness, as measured by Sachs and Warner (1995). A country with poor policies would be one with high inflation, large fiscal imbalances, and a closed trade regime (Nicaragua in the 1980s, for instance). An example of good economic policy would be Uganda in the mid-1990s.

The measure of institutional quality involves an assessment of the strength of the rule of law, the quality of public bureaucracy, and the pervasiveness of corruption. As the crisis of 1997–98 has shown, Indonesia is a country with poor institutional quality. Botswana, with its high-quality institutions, is a different story.

As donors make more of an effort to support good management, they likely will want to broaden the measure beyond the macroeconomic and institutional features illuminated here. For example, efforts to improve education and health are critical for successful development. And government support to agricultural research and extension and to community solidarity efforts made an important contribution to East Asia's success (Ishikawa 1960, 1978). The general point is that the definition of "good management" emerges from the actual experiences of developing countries.

- Providing access through the primary health care system to reproductive health services for all women and girls of child-bearing age as soon as possible and no later than 2015.
- Implementing national strategies for sustainable development in all countries by 2005 to ensure that losses of environmental resources are reversed both nationally and globally by 2015.

Box 4   Functions of the Development Assistance Committee

SINCE ITS INCEPTION IN 1960, THE OECD's Development Assistance Committee (DAC) has functioned as the principal strategy-setting and policy and performance review organ of the major bilateral donors.

Bilateral aid programs are not conceived and implemented in a political vacuum. Indeed they are subject to considerable domestic pressures from political and commercial interest groups in the donor countries. And bilateral aid agencies can be subject to the same kinds of disbursement-driven dynamics as multilateral development banks, creating incentives for staff to be approval-focused rather than result-focused. They can also be more concerned to show the national flag on their development projects than to join collective sector improvement efforts in which donor identities are merged.

The DAC has been the forum where the major donors have worked to keep their programs focused on development objectives, to promote coordination, and to review aid effectiveness. Every three years, each DAC member is subject to an examination of its aid policies and performance by the other members of the Committee, based on studies by the OECD staff and led by two specially designated "examiners" drawn from the Committee. These Development Cooperation Reviews, including the conclusions reached by the DAC, have been published since 1994.

Over the last decade and a half, the DAC has codified and published a comprehensive set of Principles for Effective Aid. These guidelines and best practices cover key policy orientations and operational issues in central areas of aid management such as coordination, project assistance, program assistance, technical assistance, procurement, and evaluation—as well as for such basic dimensions of development as participation and good governance, environment, and gender equality.

The DAC's Working Party on Aid Evaluation brings together the heads of the evaluation units of bilateral and multilateral development agencies to work on evaluation capacities in developing countries.

At the strategic level, the DAC produced in 1996 the report, *Shaping the 21st Century: the Role of Development Cooperation,* which provides the basis for the kind of partnerships most likely to produce development progress: on the side of the developing country, a strong commitment to an effective policy environment and key development priorities aimed at pro-poor growth; and on the donor side, increased financial support for such policies on a program and budget level combined with an emphasis on participation and capacity-building (facilitating the transfer of "knowledge and ideas").

Source: Contributed by DAC staff.

These goals are elaborated on in *Shaping the 21st Century: The Role of Development Cooperation,* produced by the Development Assistance Committee (box 4).

All this points to a different role for aid. Development assistance is more about supporting good institutions and policies than providing capital. Money is important, of course, but effective aid should bring a package of finance and ideas—and one of the keys is finding the right combination of the two to address different situations and problems.

Money Matters—In a Good Policy Environment

Aid has a large effect when countries have sound management.

Figure 4 Per Capita GDP Growth in Low-Income Countries with Sound Management

Annual percentage growth

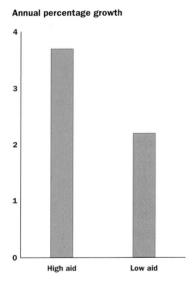

Source: Burnside and Dollar 1998.

S O, GIVEN THE NEW PATH IN DEVELOPMENT THINKING, WHAT IS important for long-term growth? Stable macroeconomic environments, open trade regimes, and protected property rights, as well as efficient public bureaucracies that can deliver education, health, and other public services. When developing countries have this kind of sound management, financial aid has a big effect on growth and poverty reduction, improving social indicators over and above what good management itself induces. Equally, aid has little effect on the development of countries with poor management. Financial aid will have a lasting effect only in a healthy climate for efficient investment and human capital development. Three sources provide the evidence—cross-country studies, research into the success and failure of investment projects financed by the World Bank, and case studies of aid effectiveness.

Few cross-country studies have found a robust effect of aid on growth. The picture changes, however, if countries are distinguished according to their economic management. Aid generally has a large effect in good-management environments: 1 percent of GDP in assistance translates to a sustained increase in growth of 0.5 percentage points of GDP. Some countries with sound management have received only small amounts of aid and have grown at 2.2 percent per capita. The good-management, high-aid group, however, grew much faster—3.7 percent per capita (figure 4). There is no such difference for countries with poor management. Those receiving small amounts of aid have grown sluggishly (if at all), as have those receiving large amounts. Introducing other variables does not change the picture.

The effect of aid goes beyond growth. In a country with sound management, 1 percent of GDP in assistance reduces poverty by 1 percent. Aid has a similar effect on infant mortality, but again only if there is good management.

A final lesson from cross-country studies is that, with sound country management, aid works in partnership with private capital. Specifically, 1 percent of GDP in aid crowds in another 1.9 percent of GDP in private investment. Put another way, assistance to well-managed countries increases private sector confidence and supports important public services. It hardly needs to be said, but in poorly managed countries aid crowds out private investment.

More evidence on the relationships among aid, management, and development comes from analysis of the success and failure of public

Figure 5 Project Performance by Policy and Institutional Environment

Projects perform better with better policies and better institutions.

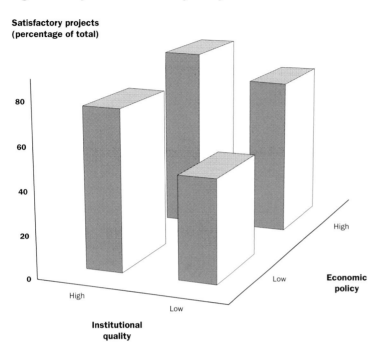

Satisfactory projects
(percentage of total)

Source: World Bank 1997a.

investment projects financed by the World Bank—in, for example, roads, power, and education. In countries with good macroeconomic management and efficient public institutions, projects were 86 percent successful, with much higher rates of return. In countries with weak policies and institutions, the corresponding figure is a measly 48 percent (figure 5).

Case studies of aid effectiveness have come to similar conclusions. Again, look at some earlier comparisons: the important role of aid to Bolivia after it reformed, compared with the largely ineffective aid to Nicaragua, which had poor policies throughout the 1980s; or the highly effective aid to Botswana (one of the countries with the best institutions and policies) in contrast to the many failures in Tanzania.

While it is useful as an illustration to draw a sharp distinction between good and bad management, there is in fact a continuum of policy regimes. Many developing countries fall into a gray area between good management and poor. The key recommendation from these findings is not that finance should go only to well-managed countries. Rather, we recommend that aid be allocated on the basis of poverty and economic management.

Being a former colony attracts more aid than having good policies.

Figure 6 Bilateral Aid and Colonial Past

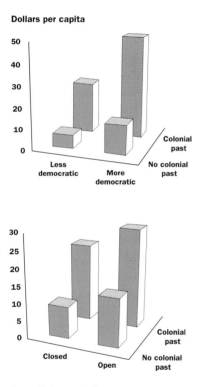

Source: Alesina and Dollar 1998.

Among countries with similar poverty levels but different policy regimes, more finance should go to the countries with better management.

The actual allocation of aid has often been influenced by the strategic interests of donors. Although donor behavior differs, total bilateral aid has favored former colonies and political allies more than open economies or democracies. An undemocratic former colony gets about twice as much assistance as a democratic noncolony, and the same is true for a closed former colony compared with an open noncolony (figure 6). As a result, much bilateral aid has gone to countries with poor management. Indeed, countries with poor management have received about the same amount of bilateral aid as countries with good management (after controlling for per capita income and population).

Aggregating the flows from different donors obscures the different criteria on which aid is allocated. In the Nordic countries, strategic variables—such as a colonial past or United Nations voting patterns—play almost no part in allocations. Nordic aid is targeted to the poorest countries, favoring open economies and democracies. Multilateral assistance has been more effectively targeted than bilateral assistance to countries with sound management, though there is still room for improvement. Overall, aid is more effective at promoting growth and reducing poverty when it is channeled to poor countries with sound management. A $10 billion increase in aid would lift 25 million people per year out of poverty—if it favors countries with sound management. By contrast, an across-the-board increase would lift only 7 million out of poverty.

There are two reasons to be optimistic that foreign aid can be allocated more efficiently in the future. First, the end of the Cold War reduces the pressure to provide aid to strategic allies. In a few highly distorted economies (Myanmar, Nigeria, Zaire) aid declined dramatically in the early 1990s. Second, there has been a worldwide trend toward economic reform in developing nations. Thus, a growing number of very poor countries have relatively good policies. Ethiopia, India, Uganda, and Vietnam, for instance, have large populations and many poor people, but have made great strides in economic reform in recent years. Aid targeted to such low-income reformers can have a big effect on growth and poverty reduction. By the same token, large amounts of finance cannot be put to productive use before countries reform. In the highly distorted environments, donors need to find other instruments to support development

Aid Can Be the Midwife of Good Policies

ORE THAN JUST PROVIDING MONEY, FOREIGN AID MUST promote sound policies and help develop institutions. Recent literature shows that policy reforms that are not difficult technically (stabilization and trade liberalization) can add 2–3 percentage points to developing countries' growth. Since average developing country growth has been only 1 percent per capita, that would be a huge improvement.

Policy reforms depend mainly on domestic political and social factors.

Much development assistance is aimed at promoting policy reform, and the record is mixed. Such reforms depend mainly on domestic political and social factors, which are not easy for outsiders to influence. But where development assistance to highly distorted regimes has stimulated policy reform, the nonfinancial aspect of aid has often been the important factor. Thus it is possible for donors to make headway in promoting policy reform in difficult environments without violating the first recommendation—that is, give more money to good policy performers. In poor policy environments, ideas are more important than money.

Some of the most important ways in which foreign assistance promotes policy reform are hard to measure. There has been a worldwide trend toward economic liberalization in the 1990s, and dissemination by development agencies of ideas about good policy has surely had an influence. Donors and foundations have also played an important role in financing the overseas education of policymakers. The Berkeley-trained group that designed Indonesia's reform package in the 1970s is a classic example. Many of Latin America's impressive reforms in the 1980s and 1990s were engineered by politicians and officials with advanced training that was partly financed by aid.

Some efforts may pay off only over a long period. In the early 1990s, for example, the World Bank launched a public education campaign in Ukraine to stimulate debate within civil society about economic reform. Ukraine has yet to achieve really good policies, but the support to popular education may yet have a big payoff. It is difficult to measure the precise effects of disseminating knowledge, educating officials, and stimulating popular debate. Case studies suggest, however, that they are often important to a successful reform program.

A more straightforward way to promote policy reform through aid is to make financing conditional on the adoption of certain policies—an

New governments are more likely to reform.

Figure 7 Elections, Tenure, and Probability of Successful Reform

Probability of success (percent)

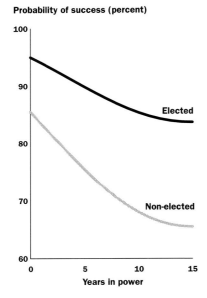

Source: Dollar and Svensson 1998.

approach long followed by the International Monetary Fund (IMF) and the World Bank. Results have been far from uniform. In many cases policy measures were not carried out, yet loans were disbursed anyway. About a third of the World Bank's adjustment loans fail in that reform objectives are not met: "policy reforms rarely succeed unless the government is genuinely convinced that the reforms have to be implemented and considers the reform program its own" (World Bank 1997a, p. 37). While results improved in the 1990s, further progress—incorporating the lessons of the recent East Asian experience—is still needed.

A recent study found that the success (or failure) of adjustment loans could largely be predicted by a country's underlying institutional and political features, including whether the leader had been democratically elected and how long the government had been in power. A newly elected reform government had a greater probability of success, than an authoritarian government in power for a long time (figure 7). In general, new governments have a high success rate with reform and are good candidates for support. This often includes governments that arise in post-conflict situations. The study also found that variables under the World Bank's control, such as the number of conditions or resources devoted to preparation and supervision, had no significant effect on the probability of success or failure of reform.

The implication: conditionality is unlikely to bring about lasting reform if there is no strong domestic movement for change. When domestic constituencies are committed to reform, adjustment loans and foreign aid can help consolidate policy gains in three ways. First, conditional loans are a means by which a reform-minded government can publicly commit to policy measures. Second, conditionality sends a signal to the private sector that a reform program is credible, and this should encourage a quicker response from investors. Third, aid spurs growth in a good policy environment. So, if reforms have moved quickly and already improved the policy environment, financial aid will have a big effect, which in turn should help sustain political support for the reforms. This is the conclusion of a review of eight successfully reforming countries in the postwar period (Sachs 1994). Sachs argues that in all cases the government was already committed to reform, but timely foreign assistance played an essential role. What aid did was to "help good governments to survive long enough to solve problems" (p. 512). Donors have gradually learned this lesson, and there is evidence that they have become more selective in providing policy-based aid: in the 1990–95 period, the success rate of World Bank adjustment loans climbed to 76 percent, compared with 67 percent before 1990 (World Bank 1997a).

Thus, in supporting policy reform, the mix and timing of ideas and finance are crucial for effective assistance. In countries without reform movements, donors can try to nurture them through analytical work, training, and technical assistance. Such nonfinancial assistance remains important as reform movements develop and consolidate reform plans. The timing of large-scale finance must also be exact. If it comes too early, the emergence of a coherent program can be undermined, and the finance is unlikely to have much effect on growth. If it comes too late, it is an opportunity missed—to increase the effect of reform on growth and to help consolidate the policy regime. In deciding timing, donors should pay attention to the progress of reform, as well as to leading indicators of successful reform (a newly elected government, for instance). Conditionality still has a role—to allow government to commit to reform and to signal the seriousness of reform—but to be effective in this it must focus on a small number of truly important measures.

Money Matters—In a Good Institutional Environment

THE COMPOSITION AND EFFICIENCY OF PUBLIC EXPENDITURES affect both growth and poverty reduction. While public provision of some services is crucial, public involvement in others is at best neutral—and at worst distorts the economy and directs attention and resources from more pressing public sector responsibilities. Although most foreign aid has financed specific investment projects, what you see is not necessarily what you get. In many cases development financing is fungible. For instance, although most aid is targeted to finance investment costs, estimates suggest that the net effect of a dollar of aid is to increase public investment by only 29 cents—exactly the amount by which any dollar of government revenue would have raised investment (figure 8). Similarly, an aid dollar used to finance projects in education tends to increase government spending in all sectors to the same extent as a dollar of government revenue from any source.

If aid resources are fungible, the effects of "money aid" and "ideas aid" need to be assessed separately. Fungibility means that a government can

A dollar of aid increases public investment by exactly the same amount as any dollar of government revenue.

Figure 8 Public Investment from One Dollar of Tax Revenue or Official Development Assistance

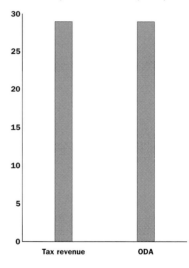

Source: Feyzioglu, Swaroop, and Zhu 1998.

Countries with public sectors that provide effective, high-quality services are prime candidates for large amounts of financial support.

use increased resources as it chooses—to increase spending, fund tax cuts, or reduce the fiscal deficit. The effectiveness of finance depends on the quality of all public investments and expenditures, not simply on aid-financed sectors and projects. This finding has important implications for the evaluation and management of aid. Agencies often hone in on the success rate of individual projects as one measure of their effectiveness. At first glance, this appears to be a focus on "quality." But it can lead to distorted incentives, depending on the criteria for judging success. Since money is often fungible, the return to any particular project financed by aid does not reveal the true effect of assistance. Moreover, if agencies are evaluated mainly on the success rate of projects (defined narrowly, without accounting for spillover benefits), managers will avoid risky, innovative projects in favor of things that are known to work. With fungibility, the impact of aid is not the same as the impact of the aid-financed project. The return on the finance depends on the overall effectiveness of public expenditures. In addition, there is the important question of how the project was done differently with donor support, compared with how it would have been done without such support.

Once fungibility is recognized, choosing the level of support and the instrument for providing assistance requires a view on the overall quality of public sector management. But how to judge the composition and efficiency of public spending? Governments need to choose expenditures carefully, with an eye toward the net impact of additional spending on growth and poverty reduction. And that depends on what the private sector would supply without government. Too many developing country budgets have been devoted to activities that have no growth potential and no effect on poverty: wasteful and inefficient public enterprises, middle-class subsidies for fuel, electricity, and more, and spending that benefits mainly the rich, such as credit subsidies and free universities. Moreover, the efficiency of government spending is at least as important as its composition. Governments should be judged not on how much they spend but on how much they accomplish.

Countries with public sectors that provide effective, high-quality services are prime candidates for large amounts of financial support, and it makes sense to provide some of this as general financing of the budget. This approach recognizes the reality of fungibility and economizes on the cost (both to donors and recipients) of delivering aid. Studies of foreign aid have long pointed to the problem of poor coordination among donors and the burden that this imposes on developing countries. Delivering more finance as general support to the budget would alleviate this problem.

As noted, many low-income countries fall into a gray area between good and poor management. Because implementing macroeconomic and trade reforms is technically easier than strengthening institutions (such as the civil service and the rule of law), these countries will often have relatively good macroeconomic policies but inefficient service delivery. Thus there will have to be more support for building institutions and implementing reforms in different sectors—more ideas, less money. A greater share of financing should come through projects whose value added is measured by the degree to which design and implementation helped improve performance in those sectors.

Finally, donors should be more willing to cut back financing to countries with persistently low-quality public sectors. While it is difficult to withdraw support, attempts to work around a poor-quality public sector are unlikely to produce anything worthwhile or lasting. In these cases donor support should be geared less to financing and more to activities that in the long run may lay the groundwork for institutional and policy reform—again, back to ideas, with only enough finance to put the new ideas to work. The general point is that different country environments require different instruments of support.

Donors should be more willing to cut back financing to countries with persistently low-quality public sectors.

Aid Can Be the Midwife of Good Institutions

MANY IMPORTANT PUBLIC SERVICES—SUCH AS MUCH OF BASIC infrastructure—are difficult (or impossible) to allocate through markets. But the economic characteristics that make these services candidates for government involvement also create problems in designing institutions and incentives that would make the public sector efficient. One major development challenge for 2000 and beyond is getting governments to do well the things that governments must do.

Well-designed aid can support effective public institutions and good governance by helping with the experimentation, learning, dissemination, and implementation of new ideas on service provision. Where there is demand for change, aid can make a big contribution, often through projects. As noted, the money element of a project does not necessarily stick with a particular sector because government revenues are fungible.

Beneficiary participation can quintuple project success.

Figure 9 Success in Rural Water Supply Projects with Differing Levels of Beneficiary Participation

Successful projects
(percentage of total)

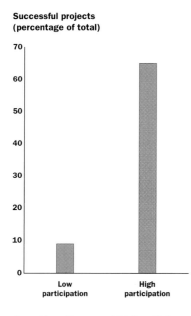

Source: Isham, Narayan, and Pritchett 1995.

Thus the main rationale of projects must be to support reform of sector institutions and policies and demonstrate new ways of achieving development results.

Various historical, legal, political, and economic conditions make each country's situation unique—and often require the generation of new knowledge. Aid can help governments by bringing to bear lessons from their own, or international, experience, and by creating conditions that help experimentation and, more important, evaluation. Aid projects can assist countries to improve the performance of entire sectors.

Unfortunately, aid has sometimes been part of the problem. Past aid has gone almost exclusively to (or through) central governments and has affected how public services are delivered. Even though some local governments can provide services more effectively, developing countries tend to have unnecessarily centralized service provision, to which aid has contributed. The traditional design and management of aid packages have also reduced the participation of local communities in the design and implementation of development projects.

Donor responses to weak institutions have in the past often been ineffective. Faced with low implementation capacity and pressure to "move the money," aid agencies have a long history of attempting to "cocoon" their projects using free-standing technical assistance, independent project implementation units, and foreign experts—rather than trying to improve the institutional environment for service provision. In many cases these efforts have been as much, or more, of a failure as efforts to induce macroeconomic policy reform. They have neither improved services in the short run nor led to institutional changes in the long run.

Aid can help improve institutions and policies at the sector level in many ways:

- Analytical work of donor agencies, such as the World Bank, has been shown to increase the probability of success of public projects. In one study an additional $10,000 in analytical work returned $80,000 in stronger benefits from projects.

- In a sample of donor-financed rural water supply projects, the success rate was 68 percent for projects with high beneficiary participation, but only 12 percent for projects with low participation (figure 9). More important, donor efforts to promote beneficiary participation helped the adoption of this approach to service provision.

- Comparing project success across countries shows the importance of the institutional environment for public investments. In general, more civil liberties (freedom of the press, freedom to assemble, and so on) lead to more project successes. Effective provision of community services requires that citizens' voices be heard.

■ About 40 percent of World Bank projects have had a substantial effect on institutional development—that is, they have helped change the way the public sector does business.

The findings suggest that the key role of aid projects as a way of providing development assistance is not to move money but to support the creation of an effective public sector. Aid agencies can provide ideas about how to improve services and finance innovative approaches. Learning from these innovations generates knowledge about what works and what does not. This view of development projects has important implications, not only for the choice and evaluation of projects, but for the way aid agencies are designed and evaluated. In particular, the evaluation of projects from the donors' point of view should focus on whether they had a positive impact on the institutions and policies of the sector.

Money, but More Ideas, Too

DEVELOPING COUNTRIES ARE TO A LARGE EXTENT MASTERS OF their own fate. Domestic economic management matters more than foreign financial aid. Economies that lag are held back more by policy gaps and institutions gaps than by a financing gap. Aid as money has a large impact only once countries have made substantial progress with reform of policies and institutions. Poor countries with good policies should get more aid than ones with mediocre policies—but in fact they get less (figure 10).

Foreign aid has concentrated too much on the transfer of capital with (often) scant attention to the institutional and policy environment into which resources were flowing. This approach resulted from misunderstandings about development—overemphasizing finance at the expense of policies and institutions—and from external and internal pressures on aid institutions. Disbursements (of loans and grants) were easily calculated and tended to become a critical output measure for development institutions. Agencies saw themselves as being primarily in the business of dishing out money, so it is not surprising that much went into poorly managed economies—with little result.

Poor countries with good policies should get more aid than ones with mediocre policies—but in fact they get less.

Figure 10 Actual Allocation of Aid, 1996, and Optimal Allocation to Reduce Poverty

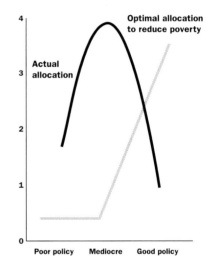

Aid (percentage of GDP)

Source: Collier and Dollar 1998.

23

So, what can the international community usefully do in highly distorted environments? Obviously there is no simple answer to this question. Almost nothing positive has happened in Burma (Myanmar) or Nigeria in the past three decades, so it would be hubris to pretend that there is some magic solution to the problems of these and similar countries. Nevertheless, there are examples of successful assistance that has improved the lives of people in such countries.

The final chapter of the report presents four case studies of effective aid under difficult conditions: adjustment without adjustment lending in Vietnam; support to education decentralization in El Salvador, Pakistan, and Brazil; a health financing innovation in Cameroon; and the

---

Box 5   Stakeholder Views on Aid Effectiveness

IN PREPARING THIS REPORT, THE MESSAGES WERE discussed with a wide range of stakeholders from the developing and developed worlds. Although there inevitably are some differences in views, the extent to which there was broad agreement on what factors account for successes in development assistance is remarkable:

Not surprising, these turn out to be a policy and institutional environment conducive to earning high returns from resources applied for development; a leading role by recipient countries in designing and managing development programs which helps elicit commitment to success and open governance to enforce accountability and prudence.

Benno Ndulu,
Head, Africa Economic Research Consortium

The new concept of "ownership," stressed in the Development Assistance Committee's new development strategy, aims to improve efficiency and efficacy by apportioning responsibility for costs and risks to those involved. The central government of the developing country has the lead role in forming development policy. In participatory development, however, citizens who participate—and bear a share of the burden— work to ensure the project's efficacy. The public draws

up plans, asks for assistance, bears some construction costs, and shares in responsibility for maintenance and management. This ensures enthusiastic public participation and maintains project sustainability.

Toru Shinotsuka,
Chief Economist, Japan's OECF

Close partnership with NGOs in development projects has proven effective in enhancing ownership and community participation, thereby promoting the sustainability of projects, especially those delivering services to (and empowering) local communities. But the willingness of both donor agencies and recipient governments to involve NGOs is crucial, and, here, the environment is mixed. Not all donors welcome a strong NGO role. Likewise, government receptiveness to NGO involvement—never mind partnership—differs from country to country. Even within countries, it can vary widely among local governments, as in the Philippines. Much advocacy work remains to be done, and the World Bank's leadership in promoting civil society partnership in development cooperation is critical.

Cielito Habito,
Secretary of Socio-Economic Planning,
Republic of the Philippines

Source: OECF/World Bank 1998, 23, 15, 21.

Africa road maintenance initiative. Running through these cases of success in the difficult environments are four themes:

- *Finding a champion.* Countries, governments, and communities are heterogeneous. While it is fair to characterize Burma overall as "poorly managed," there are likely to be reform-minded elements in the community and even in the government. If aid can find and support these reformers, it can have a big impact.

- *Having a long-term vision of systemic change.* Successful reformers have a vision of how things could be different in 10 years—different both in outcomes (more kids going to school, graduating, getting jobs) and in process (community involvement in schools, broad public support for reform policies).

- *Supporting knowledge creation.* While reformers typically have a long-term vision, they often need to develop the details of reform through innovation and evaluation. Furthermore, for reform to take root requires a demonstration that it actually works. Financing and evaluating innovations is a key role of development assistance.

- *Engaging civil society.* In the highly distorted environments, the government is failing to provide supportive policies and effective services. This is why government-to-government financial transfers produce poor results. Effective aid in this case often involves supporting civil society either to pressure the government to change or to take service provision directly into its own hands.

The foregoing points concern characteristics of promising environments for change and how donors can promote those characteristics. The lessons of successful assistance also provide guidance about donor behavior. Aid is more effective when:

- *Agencies focus on long-term reform.* It is noteworthy that success in difficult environments typically involves intensive staff input from donors and small disbursements of money. It also goes "beyond projects" to support systemic reforms. In the difficult environments, effective assistance is more about ideas than it is about money or projects. Money may be one input, as in the examples in Chapter 5. Projects can also be a useful input. But the focus of assistance in these cases was on supporting people with new ideas or looking for new ideas.

- *Donors work in partnership rather than in competition.* Studies of aid have long pointed to the proliferation of donors and lack of coordi-

For reform to take root requires a demonstration that it actually works.

In cases of successful assistance donors focus on larger transformations, not on individual projects and flags.

nation among them. Well-managed countries force coordination on donors, but in the weak environments they often run amok. It is hard to explain this behavior, except that different donors like to "plant their flags" on something tangible. In the cases of successful assistance, we tend to find strong partnership among donors with a focus on larger transformations, not on individual projects and flags.

As the focus of aid expands to money and ideas, management and evaluation become trickier. Agencies are trying to support policy reform and institutional development at both the macroeconomic and sectoral levels. The privileged units of account should be the country or sector program. Individual projects will be important in supporting sectoral development, but they should be evaluated primarily on their contribution, as building blocks and testing grounds, to the reform of sectoral institutions and policies. "Evaluating the Bank's effectiveness can no longer focus only on the project, it must also measure the impact of the full range of bank activities at the sector and country levels. This calls for new evaluation instruments and modalities . . ." (World Bank 1997a, p. 1).

Donor agencies have learned from their success and failures. In the 1990s all of the major agencies have instituted reforms aimed at strengthening the focus on results on the ground. Most agencies have also developed country assistance strategies so that individual activities now must fit into a larger game plan for policy reform and institutional change. In the same vein, the focus of evaluation has risen above the level of the project to overall country program reviews. These essentially ask: Have agencies used their resources to stimulate institutional and policy changes that have led to improved services and better quality of life? This is not an easy question to answer. But it is the right one to ask. The Overseas Development Council recently sponsored reviews of the overall impact of aid in eight African countries, conducted jointly by scholars from the developing countries in question and from major donor countries—which seems to be a fruitful approach. Similarly, the shareholders of the IMF recently turned to a group of outside scholars to assess the Fund's support to low-income reformers. And the World Bank has initiated country assistance reviews with input from a wide range of stakeholders.

Called for are independent reviews of development agencies with strong input from developing countries and focusing on two questions: Has the bulk of financing gone to sound institutional and policy environments? And have agencies contributed to policy reform and institutional change? Evaluating the right things should feed back into the management and incentives within agencies. With better management and evaluation, development agencies should become:

- *More selective*—putting more money into economies with sound management.
- *More knowledge-based*—using resources to support new approaches to service delivery, expanding knowledge about what works, and disseminating this information as a core business.
- *Better coordinated*—results-oriented agencies should worry less about planting their flags on particular projects and more about how communities, governments, and donors working together can improve services.
- *More self-critical*—agencies should be asking themselves continually: Why do we do what we do? And what is the impact?

With a better understanding of development and aid effectiveness and with the end of Cold War strategic pressures, there is reason to be optimistic that reform of aid agencies will succeed.

There is reason to be optimistic that reform of aid agencies will succeed.

Notes

1. Even a partial list would include books by those outside aid agencies (Cassen 1986, updated in 1994; Riddell 1996; Mosley 1987; Krueger, Michalopoulos, and Ruttan 1989), various institutional evaluations, and large bibliographies on specialized topics, such as aid and macroeconomics (White 1992), policy-based lending (Killick 1991), aid and nongovernmental organizations (Riddell, Bebbington, and Peck 1995), and aid and post-conflict reconstruction (World Bank 1998b).

2. Because of data availability, the focus of this study is assistance from OECD countries to the developing world. It does not cover South-South aid (for example, from Kuwait or Saudi Arabia) or the Soviet Union's extensive foreign aid.

3. The report focuses on international efforts to support long-term growth and poverty reduction in the developing world. There are other important types of international cooperation not covered by the study, such as efforts to reduce cross-border narcotics traffic or to pro-

mote peaceful conflict resolution. Furthermore, humanitarian aid, which accounts for less than 10 percent of development assistance and focuses on short term mitigation efforts, is a separate issue not addressed in this report.

4. The oft-made suggestion that the early consensus was on physical investment and that the new consensus is a shift to human investment is belied by the literature and by reality. Gunnar Myrdal's classic *Asian Drama,* written in the 1950s, signaled the intellectual shift to roughly equal emphasis on physical and human capital

5. It would be wrong to be overly critical of earlier views or those who held them, as economics is an inexact science and reading the evidence is difficult. A 50-year-old development economist making policy in 1960 would have witnessed in his or her lifetime: the Great Depression, the success of World War II planning in ending unemployment and raising wartime production, the spectacular rise of the Soviet Union under central planning, and the catch-up of Japan to the European powers.

CHAPTER 1

Money Matters—In a Good Policy Environment

Many of the measures that promote long-term growth also help reduce poverty.

MANY DEVELOPING COUNTRIES HAVE RECEIVED large amounts of foreign aid over long periods. But has aid reduced poverty and infant mortality or increased per capita income and private investment? Would more effective aid raise incomes and significantly lower poverty in the future? And can aid's effect on poverty be improved by reallocating it from some countries to others?

All aid is ultimately aimed at promoting growth and reducing poverty, whatever the immediate objectives. In an ideal world, $1 million of aid to one country would have the same marginal effect on growth and poverty reduction as channeling the same amount to another country. In the real world, this does not happen. Some countries benefit more than others. Why? Aid effectiveness largely depends on the institutions and policies of recipient countries. Where economic management is sound, aid leads to higher private investment, more rapid growth, lower infant mortality, and a faster decline in poverty. Where economic management is poor, aid has little effect on development.

The next section of this chapter briefly reviews the divergent growth experiences of developing countries. Growth helps reduce poverty and improve social indicators, which is why the relationship between aid and growth is important. Then some stylized facts about growth, institutions, and policies are examined, and the question asked: why should aid affect growth? After that, we look at the relationship between aid and growth, aid and poverty reduction, and aid and private investment. Then another question: how has aid—both bilateral and multilateral—been allocated? Finally, recommendations are made on how aid can be made more effective.

Different Countries, Different Fortunes

IN 1966 ETHIOPIA, INDIA, AND THAILAND WERE ALL POOR COUNTRIES. In each society a majority of people were living on less than $1 a day (in 1985 prices). Compared with many other developing countries, India did well, doubling real per capita income between 1966 and 1990, and reducing poverty to 53 percent of the population. But over the same period Thailand did very well, tripling per capita income and cutting poverty to just 2 percent. This difference is what Robert Lucas means by the "staggering consequences for human welfare" of different rates of growth and development. The contrast between Thailand and Ethiopia is even starker. In 1966 Thailand had about four times Ethiopia's per capita income. By 1990 Ethiopians had seen no income growth, and Thailand was more than 10 times wealthier.

Growth matters not for its own sake, but because it raises living standards. Of every 1,000 babies born in 1967 in Thailand, 84 did not survive the first year of life. By 1994 that figure had been cut by nearly two-thirds. India and Ethiopia also made progress, but not as much. In India infant mortality fell by a half over this period. In Ethiopia it fell by only 27 percent. Other social indicators tell a similar story. By 1990 Thailand had achieved universal primary education for girls, while the figure for India was 91 percent and for Ethiopia, 19 percent.

Growth does not eliminate poverty and deprivation, but per capita incomes and social indicators tend to improve (or deteriorate) together: life expectancy, school enrollment, infant mortality, and child malnutrition are all closely related to per capita income. Although there have been great improvements in living standards globally, the huge differences across countries show the importance of development. Take infant mortality: in nearly every developing country it fell between 1967 and 1994. The extent of the decline, however, varied widely (figure 1.1). Economically stagnant countries such as Zaire (now Democratic Republic of Congo), Ethiopia, Niger, and Zambia saw only modest falls, while such faster-growing countries as Botswana, Chile, Lesotho, Mauritius, and Tunisia saw improvements of 70 percent or more.

Rising incomes of the poor expand their capacity to improve their health, education, and living standards. Moreover, many of the measures that promote long-term growth—basic education or an open trade regime, for example—also help reduce poverty. But economic growth does not solve all ills: environmental degradation, crime and violence,

"Rates of growth of real per capita GNP are diverse, even over sustained periods. For 1960–80 we observe, for example: India, 1.4 percent per year; Egypt, 3.4 percent; South Korea, 7.0 percent. . . . Between the 60s and 70s, Indonesia's growth increased from 3.9 to 7.5.

"I do not see how one can look at figures like these without seeing them as representing possibilities. Is there some action a government of India could take that would lead the Indian economy to grow like Indonesia's? If so, what, exactly? The consequences for human welfare involved in questions like these are simply staggering: Once one starts to think about them, it is hard to think about anything else."

Robert E. Lucas, Jr.
"On the Mechanics of
Economic Development"
p. 4–5

From the same starting points in 1967, infant mortality fell to 33 per thousand in Botswana in 1994 while remaining virtually unchanged at 110 in Zambia.

Figure 1.1 Infant Mortality in Selected Countries, 1967 and 1994

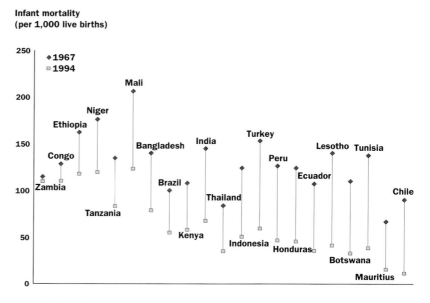

Source: *World Development Indicators 1998.*

sex discrimination, social exclusion, and the like may or may not improve with income. When people improve their status from low to middle income, new challenges emerge for society. Consider, for example, the choking haze—from fires set to clear plantations—that enveloped Southeast Asia in the summer of 1997. Or the many developing country cities that have severe problems with traffic congestion and air pollution.

Still for low-income countries, generating self-sustaining growth is a crucial first step in development. If Ethiopia's total output were divided evenly among households, everyone would be poor. Growth (an increase in per capita income) is clearly required to solve poverty and its problems: malnutrition, poor health, and lack of education and basic social services.

Overall, developing countries have made tremendous progress: more babies are surviving, more food is on the table, more children are in school, and there are fewer deaths from easily preventable diseases. There has been more global improvement in life expectancy in the past 40 years than in the previous 4,000 (World Bank 1993). The revolutionary expansion of education can be seen across generations: 62 percent of Chinese in their sixties received no schooling as children, compared with just 5 percent of young adults. In Indonesia 80 percent of 60-year-olds had no schooling, compared with just 15 percent of young adults.

But in all dimensions, progress has been uneven geographically. The greatest improvement has been in fast-growing economies. Since World War II, developing countries have fallen into three categories: fast growers, slow and stalled growers, and nongrowers and reversals (Pritchett 1998). A small but significant group—Botswana, Indonesia, the Republic of Korea, and Thailand—has grown much faster than industrial countries (table 1.1). The gap between these countries and the United States (the leader in income) has narrowed impressively.

Countries can, and do, move in (and out) of the group of fast growers. Many were sure that Korea was a basket case before growth took off in the early 1960s. Indonesia in 1966 was plagued by slow growth, high inflation, and social unrest. Before the boom in 1974, Mauritius's GDP per capita was lower than in 1960. Other countries have joined the high-growth set more recently: China since the late 1970s, and Chile since 1984. Countries also fall out of the fast-grower set. Brazil's growth was 4.2 percent from 1965 to 1980 but then –0.2 percent from 1980 to 1992. And Indonesia's growth will certainly slow as a result of its current crisis.

Slow growers, with growth rates similar to those of industrial countries, include Bangladesh, India, Malawi, and Pakistan. They have not been falling behind, but they are not catching up either. In 1990 per capita income in the United States was 18 times India's, about the same as in 1966. But since per capita income roughly doubled for each country, the absolute gap is now much wider. Slow-growing countries have seen some improvement in poverty and social indicators, but not nearly as much as the fast growers.

For a significant number of people in the world, there has been no per capita growth in recent decades, or even (especially recently) substantial decline. Many of these people live in Africa: for instance, Côte d'Ivoire, Ethiopia, and Zambia. Non-Africans include Haitians, Nicaraguans, and Iranians. In relative terms, these countries are falling further behind the rest of the world. In 1966 per capita income in the United States was 20 times Zaire's; now it is 50 times.

Table 1.1 Real Per Capita Income Relative to the United States

	Percentage of U.S. income	
	1966	1990
Fast growers		
Botswana	4.7	12.5
Indonesia	5.0	10.9
Korea, Rep. of	9.6	37.0
Thailand	10.1	19.8
Slow growers		
Bangladesh	8.8	7.7
India	5.4	7.0
Malawi	3.6	2.9
Pakistan	7.3	7.7
No growers		
Côte d'Ivoire	11.6	6.7
Ethiopia	2.4	1.8
Haiti	7.3	4.5
Iran	29.0	18.8
Nicaragua	18.7	7.2
Zaire	5.1	2.2
Zambia	8.5	3.8

Source: Summers and Heston 1991.

Why the Divergence?

There is plenty of evidence that good macroeconomic management provides a fertile environment for growth.

HOW TO EXPLAIN THESE WIDELY DIFFERING GROWTH PERFOR-mances? It was once thought that the key factor holding back poor countries was a lack of savings and foreign exchange for investment. Part of the initial rationale for foreign aid was to help countries overcome a "savings gap" to finance necessary investment and a "foreign exchange gap" so that imported machinery could be the cornerstone of that investment. Development agencies worked with a "two gap" model that made imports and investment in physical capital the driving force of growth. The role of aid in promoting growth was clear, since aid can help fill both gaps.

The slow stagnation and sudden collapse of the Soviet system of central planning, which was the intellectual father of "gap thinking" and development planning, made it clear that investment alone cannot guarantee growth. In the 1990s the focus of theoretical and empirical work on growth has gone deeper. Emphasis has shifted from investment to incentives. That is, from capital to the underlying institutions and policies that promote growth by encouraging efficient investment, by supporting human capital development, and by facilitating technological advance.

What are the conclusions of this new growth literature?

A stable macroeconomic climate is crucial. High inflation is bad for investment and growth (Fischer 1993). Similarly, large fiscal deficits hold back growth (Easterly and Rebelo 1993). An outward orientation and a reasonable environment for international engagement are essential: most trade liberalizations accelerate growth (Sachs and Warner 1995).[1] Fiscal, monetary, and trade policies show whether a country is well managed at the macroeconomic level, and there is plenty of evidence that good macroeconomic management provides a fertile environment for growth.

Good institutions and economic management are also needed at the microeconomic level. The strength of private property rights and the rule of law and the quality of the civil service affect long-term growth (Knack and Keefer 1995). Similarly, corruption in the public bureaucracy is bad for growth (Mauro 1995).

For their studies of aid and growth, Burnside and Dollar (1997, 1998) compiled a dataset covering 56 aid-receiving developing countries and averaging growth, aid, and other variables over four-year periods (starting with 1970–73 and ending with 1990–93). They created an economic management index based on the Sachs-Warner measure of openness, the

Figure 1.2 Economic Management and Growth in Selected Developing Countries

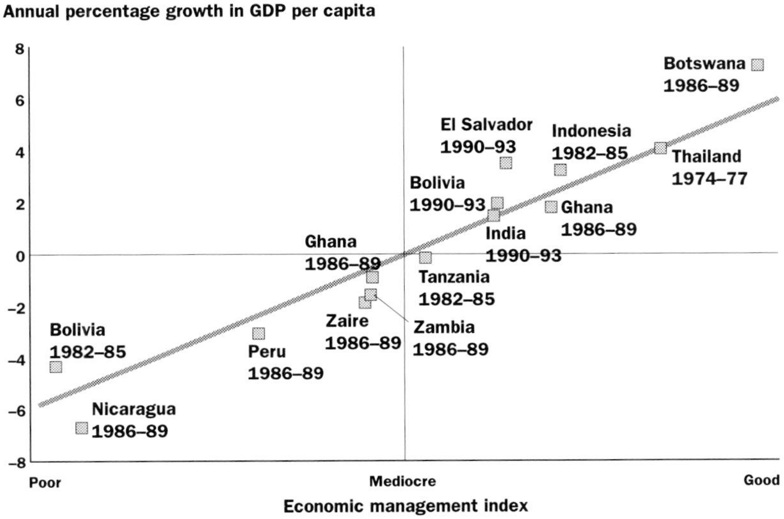

Annual percentage growth in GDP per capita

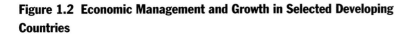

Countries with better policies can grow faster, and reform can get them there—as in Ghana and Bolivia.

Source: Burnside and Dollar 1998.

budget surplus, the inflation rate, and a measure of institutional quality. Obviously there is more to economic management, but these serve as a useful, and measurable, proxy.[2] The relationship between per capita growth and the economic management index reconfirms that sound management—at both the macroeconomic level and institutional levels—is important for growth (figure 1.2).

This finding suggests that poor countries have been held back not by a financing gap, but by an "institutions gap" and a "policy gap." If they can overcome them, they can begin to grow successfully. Botswana and Thailand are examples of good management—Tanzania and Zambia of poor. The difference in management between, say, Thailand and Tanzania may have been worth about 4 percentage points of growth. (Note that while Indonesia had solid macroeconomic policy, it scored badly on the measure of institutional quality.)

Countries can reposition themselves over time. Bolivia and Ghana had poor management in the early 1980s, but became good-management countries in the 1990s. The macroeconomic policies included in this index can be changed quickly if society and government want to reform. Other institutional aspects of good management, such as the rule of law, take longer to improve (North 1990).

33

Growth rates are also much more volatile in developing countries than in industrial countries (Easterly and others 1993). Developing countries may grow at 5 percent per capita in one four-year period, and then at –3 percent in the next. Empirical studies of growth can explain about half of the variation in growth rates among developing countries.

In Countries with Good Management . . .

Poor countries have the potential for rapid growth.

Figure 1.3 Growth Rate and Income Level

Annual percentage growth in GDP per capita

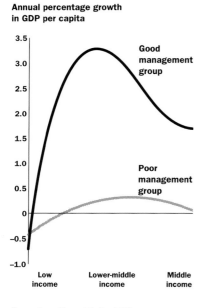

Source: Burnside and Dollar 1998.

THERE ARE POTENTIAL ADVANTAGES TO BACKWARDNESS, BUT these can be realized only with good policies (Sachs and Warner 1995). The Burnside-Dollar sample can be divided into good and poor management groups, to show the relationship between income at the beginning of a period and subsequent growth (figure 1.3). Among the good-management group, middle-income countries grow faster than high-income ones. The superstars—the East Asian tigers (before the 1997 crisis) or Chile—are found in the good-management, middle-income group, which grew much faster than high-income countries. By and large, good-management middle-income countries attract a lot of foreign direct investment, learn technologies from more advanced economies, and have investment with a high return to capital. They are catching up with the industrialized world, but as they move closer growth tends to slow, as there are fewer opportunities to learn, and the return to capital diminishes. In contrast, with poor management there is no advantage to backwardness: such countries grow slowly at all income levels. Countries that cut themselves off from globalization (through restrictive trade practices and unstable macroeconomic policies) are the biggest losers.

When low-income countries, such as Mali, put good policies in place, they perform better, but they still do not match the results for the middle-income countries. There are several reasons for this. These countries may have other characteristics that hurt growth—being landlocked, for instance. But it is also possible that their ability to save and invest is hampered by poverty itself, even when good policies are in place. If international capital markets were perfect, private money would perhaps flow to seriously reforming countries. But imperfections mean that private investors cannot accurately assess the situation and may hold back, undermining what would otherwise be a successful reform program.

This suggests a role for foreign aid in sparking developing country growth. Financial aid to poor countries that have good policies should have a high return. It can help them accelerate to rapid growth. On the flip side, there is no reason to suppose that pouring aid into poor-management countries will accelerate growth.

Development assistance can also encourage policy reforms (how it can do so is the subject of the next chapter). Serious reform can add 2–3 percentage points to growth. This would make an enormous difference in developing countries that have had little or no growth in per capita income over the past 25 years.

. . . Aid Spurs Growth

The simple relationship between aid and per capita growth in developing countries is weak, if it exists at all (figure 1.4).[3] Some countries get a great deal of assistance and grow slowly (Zambia, for instance) while others also get a lot and grow quickly (Botswana, Ghana).

From this simple starting point, there are two problems in analyzing the effect of aid on growth. First, other factors that affect growth must be

Figure 1.4 Aid and Growth in Selected Developing Countries, 1970–93

Some countries received a lot of assistance, and incomes fell—some countries received little aid, and incomes rose.

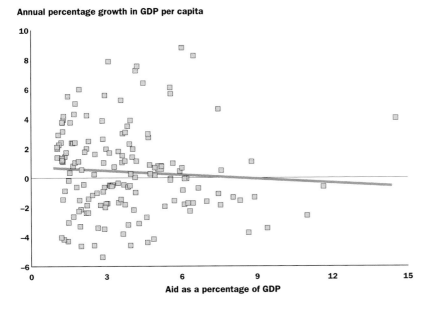

Annual percentage growth in GDP per capita

Aid as a percentage of GDP

Source: Burnside and Dollar 1998.

35

considered. Second, in some cases aid may be deliberately given to countries that are growing poorly. Consider a country hit by a typhoon that destroys the rice crop—thus reducing growth. This calamity may induce a temporary increase in aid. Thus, while the simple relationship might appear to be a negative association between aid and growth, it would be a mistake to interpret this as evidence that aid reduces growth.

A recent study addressed both of these problems and still found no relationship between aid and growth (Boone 1994). Even when a range of institutional, political, and policy variables are added to the equation the result is still the same—no relationship.

What changes the picture completely, however, is separating good-management from poor-management countries. The proposition that aid has no effect where incentives are weak was tested by Burnside and Dollar (1997). For countries with poor management it is true: whatever the amount of aid, growth was minuscule, or even negative. That some countries have received large amounts of aid for decades yet shown no growth has given aid a bad reputation.

Taking the good-management group and dividing them into high-aid and low-aid groups produces striking results. The good-management, low-aid group grew at 2.2 percent per capita, but the good-management, high-aid group grew almost twice as fast—at 3.7 percent per capita. Including other variables (institutional, political, and policy) shows that aid has a large, positive effect on growth in good-management countries (appendix 1). Removing middle-income countries, which receive little aid, from the sample makes the effect of aid even stronger. With good management, an additional 1 percent of GDP in aid increases growth by 0.5 percentage points—a rate of return of roughly 40 percent, if depreciation is 10 percent or so a year (figure 1.5). Countries with sound management that have received a lot of aid and done well include Bolivia, El Salvador, Ghana, Honduras, and Mali in the 1990s.

There are diminishing returns to aid so that—even with good management—the benefit will decline as aid is increased. However, given the amount of assistance that well-managed countries actually receive, there would still be a strong positive return to increasing aid to these countries. In Ghana in the 1990–93 period, for example, a doubling of aid would have been necessary to reach the point at which the marginal return to further finance would have been zero.

Moreover, if a country is receiving even the average amount of aid (about 2 percent of real purchasing power parity GDP), a 1 point increase

With good management an additional 1 percent of GDP in aid increases growth by 0.5 percentage point.

Figure 1.5 Marginal Impact on Growth of a Percent of GDP in Aid

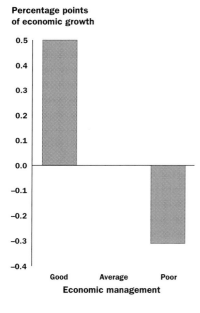

Percentage points of economic growth

Source: Appendix 1.

in its management index leads to an increase in growth of 1.3 percentage points. With twice that amount of aid the effect of good management is even stronger—growth is 1.9 percentage points higher.

Other researchers have reached similar conclusions. In a recent study comparing aid effectiveness in Bolivia, Costa Rica, and Nicaragua, Cecilia Lopez, Colombia's Minister of Planning, found that aid did not have much effect on growth in Nicaragua because of the country's highly distorted policies—a large fiscal deficit and high inflation. Aid was largely effective in Bolivia, which successfully completed a reform program in the 1980s. Lopez's conclusion from the three case studies:

Policies have a critical influence on the effectiveness of aid, for the same reasons that they affect economic growth.

- Foreign aid in itself is neutral with respect to development, for its positive or negative effects depend on government policies. Effects on economic development will tend to be positive when aid is used to build up capital or to finance public investment that contributes to the profitability of private capital, or for human capital development.
- Fiscal policy should generate government's current savings, so that both domestic and foreign resources finance public investment. If this does not happen, foreign resources may end up financing the government's current expenses and not investment projects, as happened in Nicaragua.
- The relationship between aid's positive effects and good domestic policies always holds, even during adjustment (Lopez 1997).

A study of seven African countries by researchers from donor and recipient countries (under the auspices of the Overseas Development Council) pointed to good economic policies as a key precondition for successful assistance:

"Clearly, the large influx of aid has not fostered rapid economic growth in most African countries and has been only partly successful in poverty alleviation. How can one reconcile this lack of success with the field-level evidence just cited and reach a clear verdict on aid's economic impact? Unfortunately, a number of factors prevent the establishment of a clear link between aid and the overall performance of the economy. First, government economic policies themselves can prevent aid from having the impact it otherwise would have. Policies have a critical influence on the effectiveness of aid, for the same reasons that they affect economic growth;

37

economic policies that engender balance of payments difficulties, high budget deficits, or high rates of inflation are likely to foster a climate of economic uncertainty, which dampens the private sector's response to the public investment represented by aid. A classic example of such a phenomenon is an aid-funded agricultural extension project that does not achieve its objectives of output or productivity growth, because macroeconomic policies have resulted in an overvalued exchange rate, which makes the farmer's output noncompetitive. Similarly, policies that create extensive market distortions are likely to undermine the quality of scarce resource use, resulting in socially suboptimal outcomes. Taking up the example of the agricultural extension project, farmer response is muted because the government's agricultural policies provide farmers with disincentives to adopt yield-enhancing new technologies. These are not fortuitous examples: by the mid-1980s, most experts were convinced that donor and government attempts to expand and modernize agriculture in many African states had been largely undone by macro and sectoral policies that were exacerbating the impact of the decline in world prices for agricultural commodities. They credited the prevailing policy environment with the superior performance of the agricultural sector in Kenya, for example, and the poor performance in Tanzania and Zambia" (van de Walle and Johnston 1996, p. 36–37).

In declining economies an average drop of 7 percent in per capita income led to an increase in poverty of 19 percent.

Figure 1.6 Economic Growth and Poverty

Percent

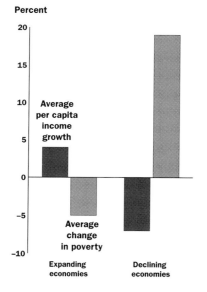

Source: Ravallion and Chen 1997.

. . . Aid Reduces Poverty

The main aim of aid is to reduce poverty. Poverty reduction in developing countries is closely related to per capita income growth. Development economists used to worry that the benefits of growth would be undone by increases in income inequality as poor countries developed. Recent evidence has shown conclusively, however, that this is not so.

One study examined trends in the distribution of income for 45 countries for which high-quality household income or expenditure data are available over time (Li, Squire, and Zou 1998). In 29 countries there has been no trend in either direction. The remaining 16 countries are divided: 8 have shown rising inequality, 8 declining. If income distribution does not change much over time, the gains in per capita income will affect different segments of society to about the same degree. Thus, in countries with rapid growth, incomes of the poorest will rise rapidly and the incidence of poverty will decline. But in countries with no per capita growth and a stable income distribution, there will be no poverty reduction.

Another study examined recent per capita growth and poverty reduction in 67 countries for which household data were available. It found that every country with increasing per capita household income saw poverty decline, and every country with declining per capita income saw poverty increase. In the expanding economies, per capita income grew 4 percent, and poverty declined 5 percent. In declining economies an average drop of 7 percent in per capita income led to an increase in poverty of 19 percent (figure 1.6).

Poverty data are not available for all countries and time periods in the Burnside and Dollar study, so direct examination of the effect of aid is impossible. But according to Bruno, Ravallion, and Squire (1998), on average a 1 percent increase in per capita income in developing countries reduces poverty by 2 percent. Put another way, in countries with sound management an extra 1 percent of real GDP in aid results in a 0.5 percentage point increase in growth and hence a 1 percent decline in poverty. In countries with poor management the expected effect of aid on poverty reduction is far less.

Aid can affect well-being in many ways. Consider changes in infant mortality, an important social indicator for which data are widely available. Burnside and Dollar found that aid helps reduce infant mortality if a country has good management—an extra 1 percent of GDP in aid leads to a decline in infant mortality of 0.9 percent (figure 1.7). In contrast, if a country has poor management, there is no marginal impact from another 1 percent of GDP in aid.

. . . Aid "Crowds in" Private Investment

The impact of aid on growth in good-management countries is high. This may be because once good management is in place, there are high-productivity public investments to be financed by aid. If an economy is growing rapidly, the return on investment in road rehabilitation, for example, is high. If the economy is stagnant, the return is lower or nonexistent. Similarly, economic growth makes it easier to get children into school and have a high return from this investment in human capital. In a sluggish economy the incentives to send children to school are weak. Thus, with good management in place, aid helps government make more of these high-return expenditures. Evidence at the microeconomic level supports this finding. Public investments financed by the World Bank,

With good management an extra 1 percent of GDP in aid leads to a decline in infant mortality of 0.9 percent.

Figure 1.7 Decline in Infant Mortality from a Percent of GDP in Aid

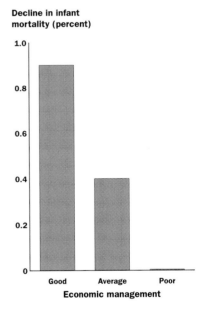

Source: Burnside and Dollar 1998.

Figure 1.8 Marginal Impact on Private Investment of a Percent of GDP in Aid

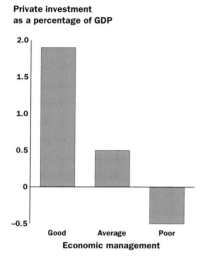

Private investment as a percentage of GDP

Economic management: Good, Average, Poor

Source: Dollar and Easterly 1998.

Figure 1.9 Bilateral, Multilateral, and World Bank Aid Per Capita and Income Level

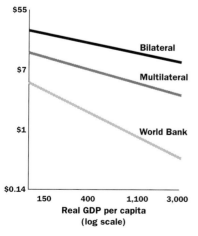

Aid per capita (log scale in dollars)

Bilateral
Multilateral
World Bank

Real GDP per capita (log scale)

Source: Calculated from Burnside-Dollar dataset.

for instance, have more success in a good institutional and policy environment: 86 percent, compared with only 48 percent in a weak institutional and policy environment (see overview figure 5).

There is another possible explanation for the relationship between aid and growth—that when a poor country puts good policies in place, domestic and foreign private investors are uncertain about the sustainability of the reform. If there is fear of reversal, investors will wait. And even with good management, low-income countries are hamstrung by other impediments, including weak infrastructure. Foreign aid to reforming governments may improve the environment for private investment—both by creating confidence in the reform program and helping to ease infrastructure bottlenecks.

In a poor-management country foreign aid may crowd out private investment: it may encourage the public sector to make commercial investments that would otherwise be undertaken by private investors. In a good-management country the effects of foreign aid would likely be magnified by crowding in private investment.

There is evidence to support these notions (Dollar and Easterly 1998). One percent of GDP in assistance increases private investment an extra 1.9 percent of GDP in good-management countries (figure 1.8). Thus the combination of good management and foreign aid is welcomed by the private sector, and this helps to explain the strong effect aid has on growth in such an environment. In a poor-management country, however, 1 percent of GDP in aid is estimated to reduce private investment by 0.5 percent of GDP, which may explain why the net effect of such aid is small.

These findings for the effect of aid on growth and private investment shed some light on the problems of the Heavily Indebted Poor Countries and how they can be helped (box 1.1).

Aid Has Not Favored Countries with Good Management

TARGETING ASSISTANCE TO POOR COUNTRIES WITH SOUND institutions and policies will make the most of scarce aid resources to encourage investment, spur growth, and reduce poverty. But between 1970 and 1993 aid allocations—by bilateral and multilateral donors—were dominated by politics—both the international politics of the Cold War and the internal politics of aid agencies.

Foreign aid is targeted to poor countries—but imperfectly. Bilateral aid per capita received by developing countries has a weak, negative relationship with their per capita income (figure 1.9). Generally, a doubling of per capita income leads to a 33 percent reduction in aid. But the behavior of bilateral donors varies widely (Ehrenpreis 1997). Half of all Swedish aid has gone to the poorest 12 percent of countries (weighted by population); of all bilateral aid, only 20 percent went to these countries. Another study also found that Canadian, Dutch, and Nordic assistance is sharply targeted to poor countries (Alesina and Dollar 1998). The relationship between aid per capita and income is stronger for multilateral aid than for bilateral and stronger still for the World Bank's International Development Association (IDA) facility, which is part of multilateral aid. For IDA, a doubling of per capita income has been associated with a 90 percent reduction in aid per capita.

Another important factor in aid allocation is population. Countries that have small populations get more assistance per capita or more rela-

---

Box 1.1   Aid and Heavily Indebted Poor Countries

HEAVILY INDEBTED POOR COUNTRIES ARE LOW-income countries that have debt they cannot service. The problem arises not largely from foreign aid (which is mostly grants), but because these countries borrowed too much from private capital markets or from official sources at near-commercial interest rates. How did they get into such trouble? And how can they be helped?

These countries had poorer management in the 1970s and 1980s than other low- income countries, and showed virtually no per capita growth in 1970–93. Even so, they were able to run up large amounts of debt. These borrowings were not put to good use and certainly did not generate a high enough return to repay the loans.

In the 1990s highly indebted poor countries have been receiving extraordinary amounts of aid to service these debts—about twice as much as they should have, based on per capita income, population, policies, and so on. Despite the assistance to service these debts, the large debt overhang creates an uncertainty

for the whole economy. What happens if donors lose interest in these extraordinary aid allocations to service debt?

The World Bank, the IMF, and other donors have started an initiative to forgive large amounts of this debt, which should give these countries more resources to provide important public services. An additional benefit of debt relief will be to improve the climate for private investment. Removing the unpayable debt, once and for all, will relieve uncertainty. Benefits from debt relief will be greater if countries have undone the poor management practices that contributed to their troubles in the first place. Debt relief is a form of aid and will have a greater impact in a good-management country. Removing the debt overhang for those with poor management is not likely to produce significant benefits. For these reasons, the debt reduction initiative for heavily indebted countries requires a track record of policy reform. The first countries to benefit from debt reduction in the mid-1990s—Uganda, Bolivia—successfully reformed policy.

Figure 1.10 Aid and Population

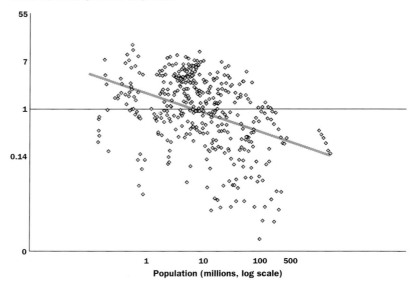

Source: Calculated from Burnside-Dollar dataset.

tive to GDP (figure 1.10). This makes sense for some assistance. For instance, it costs about the same to provide technical assistance to the central bank of India as to the central bank of Lao PDR. But if aid is financing public services, such as education or road construction, there perhaps should not be such discrimination against large countries. More than half the world's poor live in India and China: in 1990–93 they received $2 and $1 per capita in aid. Yet small countries often receive $50 per capita or more. This discrimination against large countries is one reason the relationship between aid allocation and income is not strong.

A second factor that undermines this relationship is that aid allocation often depends on the political or strategic interests of donors—for example, U.S. aid in the Middle East or European aid to former colonies. Burnside and Dollar (1997) found that political factors help explain the allocation of bilateral aid, but that multilateral aid is not strongly influenced. These factors are not important for only a handful of bilateral donors—Canada, Denmark, Finland, Netherlands, Norway, and Sweden (Alesina and Dollar 1998).

The dual objectives—pursuing strategic goals and rewarding good policies—work against each other. This can be seen by looking at the correlation between bilateral aid and management (figure 1.11). So, how have bilateral donors treated two countries with the same income and population but different management? Good and bad management regimes have received roughly the same average assistance. Being a former colony of a major donor is more valuable in attracting bilateral assistance than having good management (Alesina and Dollar 1998).

The allocation of multilateral aid has depended on income, population, and good management. Political and strategic considerations were not significant. Thus, for multilateral aid, lower-middle income countries with good management received 30 percent more than the typical poor-management country with the same income and population (figure 1.12). For very low-income countries the difference between good management and poor management has been minor.

Since most official development assistance is bilateral, the allocation of all aid together (multilateral and bilateral) shows little relationship with the quality of country management. Cold War aid driven by strategic considerations may have accomplished its political goals, but aid that went to countries with poor management did little to reduce poverty.

Figure 1.11 Allocation of Bilateral Aid, 1970–93

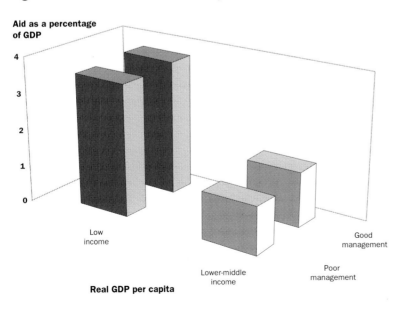

Source: Calculated from the Burnside-Dollar dataset.

Be Focused

CLEARLY, DEVELOPMENT ASSISTANCE NEEDS TO BE MORE CONCENtrated on where it can be most effective in reducing poverty. It needs to take more account of the environment in which it is placed. Finance is most effective in reducing poverty in those countries that have both mass poverty and a good policy and institutional environment. Conversely, it is less effective in countries that already have relatively little poverty, or have poor policies and weak institutions.

But is there much scope for a more focused approach? Perhaps mass poverty is so strongly linked with poor policies and weak institutions that we just don't find the combination of mass poverty and good policies in which aid is highly effective? Not so. At the moment plenty of countries combine mass poverty with good policies and institutions. Why? Because of the wave of policy reform and institution building that has swept through poor countries during the 1990s.

Figure 1.13 classifies 113 developing countries based on their incidence of poverty and the quality of their policies in 1996.[4]

What creates a great opportunity for foreign aid is the upper-right-hand quadrant. Thirty-two countries have poverty rates above 50 per-

Figure 1.12 Allocation of Multilateral Aid, 1970–93

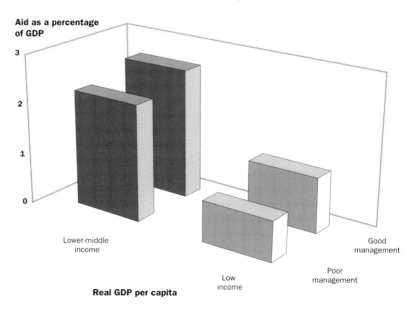

Source: Calculated from Burnside-Dollar data set.

cent, and also have above average policies. In such conditions aid is highly effective in reducing poverty. Some of the countries in this quadrant are among the poorest in the world: for example, Ethiopia, Uganda, Mali, and India. This is the *High Impact* quadrant for aid.

Conversely, in the bottom-left-hand quadrant aid is radically less effective. Sixteen countries already have a low incidence of poverty, as well as below average policies. There are fewer poor people to help, and aid does less for them because it is handicapped by the poor policies.

In the remaining two quadrants aid is less effective than in the *High Impact* quadrant.

In the upper-left-hand quadrant there are 32 countries with poverty rates above 50 percent. There are millions of poor people in these economies in need of help, but unfortunately the policy environments are not good enough for aid to have much effect. The priority for the world community in these countries is to help in the domestic political and social process of policy change: that is, in contributing knowledge rather than big finance. Of course, some financial flows provide opportunities for dialogue and knowledge transfers. But aid to these economies has to be justified more for its indirect contribution to policy change than for its direct effect on poverty reduction.

Why? Because of the wave of policy reform and institution building that has swept through poor countries during the 1990s.

Figure 1.13 Poverty and Policy, 113 Developing Countries, 1996

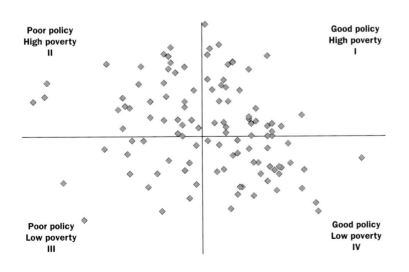

Source: Collier and Dollar 1998.

An across-the-board $10 billion increase in aid would lift 7 million people out of poverty, while a targeted increase could lift 25 million out of poverty.

In the lower-right-hand quadrant there are 31 countries that have above-average policies. Aid works in these environments, but there is less work for it to do, since there is already a low incidence of poverty.

So, there is certainly scope for a focused approach to aid: financial assistance to *High Impact* countries is far more effective than in countries in other quadrants. But is there scope for aid to be *more focused* than it is at present? Surely, donors are already taking into account poverty and policies in determining where to allocate finance—aren't they?

Actually, not very much. To see this, suppose that the world community raised an extra $10 billion and allocated it proportionately to existing aid allocations. So allocated, this extra aid could raise 7 million people out of poverty. Now suppose instead that the $10 billion were allocated to the *High Impact* quadrant. The extra impact would be dramatic: 25 million people would be raised out of poverty (Collier and Dollar 1998).

Being more focused can thus spectacularly increase the effectiveness of aid in reducing poverty. Nearly four times as many people could be lifted out of poverty for a given amount of aid. And of course, if aid became much more effective, there would be more of it. Rapid poverty reduction is the major global challenge: demonstrated effectiveness can be expected to produce greater support for aid.

Notes

1. All three of these studies consider whether good policies bring about growth or growth spurs good policies—and conclude that policy reform leads to more growth.

2. Collier and Dollar 1998 show that the finding that aid has more impact in a good management environment holds in the 1990s using a much broader measure of institutions and policies, including issues such as corruption, governance, equity, and safety nets. For research purposes, this broader measure has the disadvantage that it is not available back through time.

3. For the growth analysis, aid is measured relative to GDP at purchasing power parity (Summers and Heston 1991). In low-income countries, this measure of GDP is often three times higher than GDP at domestic prices because prices of nontraded goods tend to be low in poor countries. In the developing world the average aid receipt relative to PPP GDP is about 2 percent. The same amount would be 6–7 percent of GDP in domestic prices.

4. The measure of policy used to construct this figure is the Country Policy and Institutional Assessment of the World Bank. It has more components than the index in the Burnside-Dollar study, including such areas as social sector policies and safety nets. It has the advantage of covering a large number of countries and being up-to-date. But it is not available as a consistent measure going back in time.

CHAPTER 2

Aid Can Be the Midwife of Good Policies

SOUND MANAGEMENT THAT PRODUCES MACROECONOMIC stability, openness, rule of law, and absence of corruption leads to growth and poverty reduction. It also creates the right environment for aid to reduce poverty. While a $10 billion increase in aid could lift 25 million people out of poverty each year, an even bigger assault on global poverty will require further institution building and policy reform. Between the mid-1980s and mid-1990s there were huge advances in the quality of management in developing countries. A further improvement of the same magnitude could add a full percentage point to developing country growth and lift another 60 million people a year out of the poverty abyss. Policy reform and capacity building are the keys. Ideas and money—together—have the potential to do far more than finance alone.

In this chapter we review the relationship between aid and policy reform at the macroeconomic and sectoral levels. Has the amount of finance that countries receive affected their policies? Some conservative critiques of aid hold that finance will lead to poor policies. What is the evidence? We also examine policy-based (or conditional) lending and the extent to which it has helped improve economic policies in developing countries. Then we focus on less tangible mechanisms through which aid can affect policy—dissemination of ideas, education of future leaders, stimulation of policy debate within civil society. Arguably, this is one of the most important roles for aid.

It is hard, however, to make generalizations about aid and policy. First, it is not true that countries that receive large amounts of aid have bad policies; there is surprisingly little relationship between the amount of aid and policies. Second, policy-based lending has a mixed record. Many societies have initiated serious reform programs, and adjustment lending has been

Between the mid-1980s and mid-1990s there were huge advances in the quality of policies in developing countries.

successful in supporting those reforms and helping lock in policy gains. At the same time there is a long legacy of failed adjustment lending where there was no strong domestic constituency for reform. Foreign aid cannot take the lead in promoting reform if there is little local movement in that direction. Finally, and somewhat speculatively, case studies suggest that aid can play an important role in stimulating reform over the long haul. Foreign aid has helped finance the overseas education of many leaders, an investment that may not have much effect on policies for 20 years or more. There are also cases in which foreign assistance has stimulated policy debates within civil society, but it is difficult to measure the impact.

Conditional lending is worthwhile where reforms have serious domestic support.

Conditional lending is worthwhile where reforms have serious domestic support. As with aid in general, however, donors have not been sufficiently selective with policy-based lending. In countries with poor policies and no movement toward reform, it is worth thinking about how to create reformers and popular movements for reform, but it will not be easy. Adjustment lending has not been a useful tool in this respect, and may have been counterproductive. The role of aid in difficult environments is to educate the next generation of leaders, disseminate information about policy, and stimulate public debate where possible.

Money—Good or Bad for Reform?

SOCIAL SCIENTISTS HAVE LONG DEBATED THE ROLE OF OFFICIAL AID in supporting reform. If policy reforms have short-term costs affecting particular segments of the population, foreign aid can help get those reforms off the ground. Stabilization typically requires fiscal adjustments that lead to higher taxes or fewer services for some groups. Trade liberalization hurts firms and workers in previously protected industries. State enterprise reform and privatization often lead to transitional unemployment. If a government wants to implement these reforms, foreign aid can help with adjustment costs.

One recent study analyzed eight major postwar economic reformers: Bolivia, Chile, Germany, Israel, Mexico, Poland, and Turkey (Sachs 1994). In each case aid was a crucial contributor, though all governments were committed to reform before large-scale aid arrived. The study concluded that aid helps "good governments to survive long enough to solve problems" (p. 512). Moreover, foreign aid increases the effect of policy reform on growth, thus raising benefits relative to costs. This should increase the likelihood that reform will be sustained.

Another study, however, points out that "aid can also help bad governments to survive" (Rodrik 1996). "For debating purposes, one can cite at least as many cases as Sachs does to demonstrate an association between plentiful aid and *delayed* reform . . . . One of the pieces of conventional wisdom about the Korean and Taiwanese reforms of the 1960s is that these reforms took place in large measure because U.S. aid, which had been plentiful during the 1950s, was coming to an end" (p. 31).

Burnside and Dollar examined the relationship between aid and their index of macroeconomic and trade policies for the 56 countries in their sample. They showed first that policies can largely be explained by underlying country characteristics, such as the rule of law, ethnic splits (which are associated with poor policies), or political instability (also linked to poor policies). When aid is added to this analysis, it has no effect on the policy index. This does not refute Sachs's view that aid contributed to reform in some cases—instead, it shows only that aid supported governments with bad policies to about the same extent that it supported reforming governments.

While there is not much relationship between the amount of aid that countries get and the *level* of their policies, it is still possible that aid supports changes in policies. If donors were good at anticipating "turning points" and at increasing their aid *just before* reform, we would observe aid flowing to poor policy regimes, but the flows would be followed by reform. Alesina and Dollar (1998) investigate this possibility. In a sample of 60 countries, they identify 87 episodes in which there is a surge in aid (a large change relative to what the country had been receiving). In only six of the 87 episodes was the surge followed by significant reform. In 92 cases in which there was a large decline in aid, 16 were followed by reform. Thus, reform is more likely to be preceded by a decline in aid than an increase in aid. But the main thing that emerges from this work is that there is little relationship between changes in aid and policy reform. It is not generally the case that donors have successfully anticipated "turning points" and increased their assistance in advance of reform.

The varied relationship between aid and policy can be seen in individual countries. Zambia, for example, could support the view that aid enables governments to delay reforms. Policies in Zambia were poor and getting poorer throughout 1970–93, yet the amount of aid that it

Aid supported governments with bad policies to about the same extent that it supported reforming governments.

*In Zambia, policies got
worse while aid
increased . . .*

Figure 2.1 Zambia: Aid and Policy

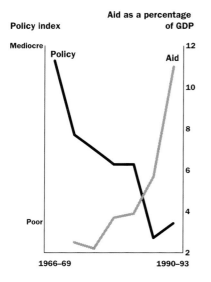

Source: Dollar and Easterly 1998.

received rose continuously—reaching 11 percent of real GDP by the
early 1990s (figure 2.1).

For every Zambia, however, there is a Ghana. Ghana received little
aid when it had bad policies—but has received strong donor support
since it reformed (figure 2.2). Case studies of Ghana generally find that
foreign assistance helped consolidate a good reform program. In
Burnside and Dollar's 56 country sample, these different experiences
cancel out: aid and policy are virtually uncorrelated. When other variables known to affect policy are introduced, there is still no relationship
between aid and policy.

So, there is no simple relationship between the amount of aid that
countries receive and the quality of their policies. Aid may still have contributed to policy reform in some cases, however, either through the leverage of conditionality or through the dissemination of ideas.

Ownership—What Money Cannot Buy

IF AID IS AS LIKELY TO DELAY REFORM AS ENCOURAGE IT, WHY NOT
make assistance conditional on policy reform? After all, financial support from the International Monetary Fund and structural adjustment lending from the World Bank are designed to disburse only as
reform measures are carried out. Although these flows are only a fraction
of official finance, other donors pay attention to structural adjustment
programs when making decisions about aid allocations.

For various reasons, however, conditionality may fail to generate permanent improvements in policy. First, it is inherently difficult to monitor. Take, for example, a seemingly simple condition: that the fiscal deficit
not exceed a certain level. The fiscal deficit is influenced not just by government policy, but by shocks outside government control. So a country
may miss an agreed target because of a shock; in fact, doing so may be
desirable because a target that is good policy in one environment becomes
poor policy in another. Whether or not a policy target has been met
requires some subjective judgment. The subjectivity becomes more acute
as reforms become more complex institutionally.

The second problem with conditionality is that it has force only during the life of the adjustment program. A government in financial diffi-
culty may agree to reforms and carry them out to obtain conditional

resources. If there is no strong commitment to these reforms, they can — and likely will—be reversed at the end of the program.

The third and probably most serious problem concerns incentives within donor agencies. Disbursing funds is one of the important rationales for these agencies. Since monitoring policy reform requires some subjective judgment, donors will likely find that governments are making a good effort—whether they are or not—and disburse their funds. *The Economist* describes this kind of donor behavior as follows:

> "Over the past few years Kenya has performed a curious mating ritual with its aid donors. The steps are: one, Kenya wins its yearly pledges of foreign aid. Two, the government begins to misbehave, backtracking on economic reform and behaving in an authoritarian manner. Three, a new meeting of donor countries looms with exasperated foreign governments preparing their sharp rebukes. Four, Kenya pulls a placatory rabbit out of the hat. Five, the donors are mollified and the aid is pledged. The whole dance then starts again" (August 19, 1995, p. 37).

There is a mountain of literature on structural adjustment lending and its effect on policies (for example, Mosley 1987, Mosley and others 1995, and Thomas 1991). All the studies conclude with skepticism about the ability of conditionality to promote reform in countries where there is no strong local movement in that direction. One concludes that, in Africa, structural adjustment lending from the World Bank affected the policies of recipients "a little, but not as much as the Bank hoped" (Mosley and others 1995). The main problem was that the World Bank had strong incentives to disburse funds—and thus was inclined to see a good effort even where there was none. In fact, in the authors' sample of adjustment loans, only 53 percent of loan conditions were met. Even so, almost all adjustment loans were disbursed. Zambia, for example, received 18 adjustment loans between 1966–69 and 1990–93 while its policies got worse (see figure 2.1). In Kenya the World Bank provided aid to support identical agricultural policy reforms five separate times. Each time reforms were either not implemented or later reversed. Yet all adjustment loans were disbursed. The lesson? A conditional loan is no guarantee that reforms will be carried out—or last once they are.

Yet, adjustment lending from the IMF and the World Bank has supported many successful reform programs. Bolivia is a good example of a

. . . but in Ghana, aid rose in lockstep with better policies.

Figure 2.2 Ghana: Aid and Policy

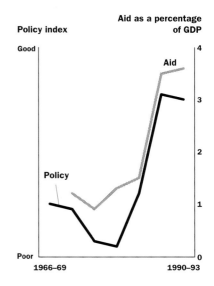

Source: Dollar and Easterly 1998.

51

In Bolivia, adjustment lending provided finance to a determined reforming government.

Figure 2.3 Bolivia: Aid and Policy

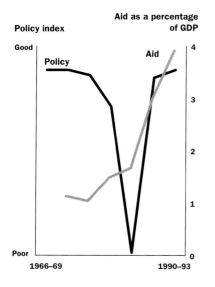

Source: Dollar and Easterly 1998.

country where adjustment lending provided finance to a determined reforming government, with assistance increasing in lock-step with policy reforms (Lopez 1997; figure 2.3). Much of this increase in finance came through adjustment loans. Another review of policy-based lending concluded: "It seems clear that the lending cum conditionality process works well only when local polities have decided, largely on their own, possibly with outside technical help, to address their reform needs, effect certain policy changes sequentially, and approach the international community for financial help in getting there" (Ranis 1995, p. 10).

In its own internal reviews the World Bank has come to the same conclusion—"ownership," or strong domestic support of reforms, is essential for adjustment lending to succeed. Before 1990 about a third of adjustment loans failed to achieve expected reforms, and the lack of borrower ownership or commitment was a key factor in the failures (Branson and Jayarajah 1995).

In a sizable sample of World Bank adjustment loans (105 cases where reforms were successfully carried out, and 55 where they were not), a recent study found several political and institutional features associated with successful reform programs (Dollar and Svensson 1997). Most important, 52 percent of governments that implemented successful reforms were democratically elected, whereas only 29 percent of governments overseeing failed programs were democratically elected. Governments that had been in power for a long time were less likely to implement reform successfully. Furthermore, political instability was highly correlated with failure (table 2.1). Political and economic variables successfully predicted the outcomes of 75 percent of the adjustment loans (appendix 2).

Table 2.1 Features of Successful and Failed Adjustment Programs

	Successful	*Failed*
Country statistics		
Democratically elected	52%	29%
Government crisis during reform period	9%	24%
World Bank variables		
Preparation (staff weeks)	143	135
Prior analytical work (staff weeks)	84	80
Number of conditions	45	47
Loan size (millions of U.S.dollars)	169	166

Source: Dollar and Svensson 1998.

The study also examined factors under the World Bank's control, including: size of the adjustment loan, number of conditions, resources used to prepare the loan, and resources devoted to analytical work in the four years prior to the loan. It found that these "Bank effort" variables are similar for successful and failed adjustment programs (see table 2.1). When all the variables are tossed into the analysis, it becomes clear that successful reform depends primarily on a country's institutional and political characteristics.

In the past the World Bank did not sufficiently take into account that success or failure of reform depends largely on a country's own effort. A case in point: Zambia. In the 1980s the Bank approved four structural adjustment loans totaling $212 million, and they were almost fully disbursed. After completion, the World Bank rated three of the four loans as failures: that is, reforms supported by the loans were not satisfactorily implemented. The Dollar-Svensson results suggest that this was largely predictable. Conditions in Zambia at the time were not conducive to reform. The government, not democratically elected and in power for a long time, was likely a nonreformer. It may have been worth taking a chance on the first adjustment loan, but (admittedly with 20/20 hindsight) a succession of policy-based loans for Zambia was not the best use of resources. Donors have gradually learned this lesson and become more selective about providing policy-based assistance. In 1990–95, the success rate of World Bank adjustment loans increased to 76 percent (World Bank 1997a).

These studies suggest that policy reform depends largely on countries' institutional and political features. Borrower ownership of reform is increasingly recognized as a prerequisite for success. But once a serious reform program is started, financial assistance can help consolidate it.

> *In the past the World Bank did not sufficiently take into account that success or failure of reform depends largely on a country's own effort.*

Fomenting Reform

EMPIRICAL LITERATURE HAS SHOWN THAT REFORMS WITHIN reach for low-income countries could add 2–3 percentage points to their growth. Given that long-term growth has been zero to 1 percent per capita for most of these countries, that would be a huge improvement. For many of the poorest countries—those that are falling further behind in relative terms—initiating serious policy reform is perhaps the most important issue on their agenda. At the same time, it is not easy to generate reform, and conditional lending into weak institutional and policy environments has failed. So, can donors promote policy reform in the highly distorted environments of, for example, Myanmar, Nigeria, or the Democratic Republic of Congo? Or do they simply throw up their arms and walk away?

Clearly, to desert difficult countries is unacceptable. As poverty is reduced in developing countries with sound policies, countries with highly distorted policies will account for an ever-increasing share of the poor. What is the answer? There is evidence that donors can make a difference without large-scale financing. Intangible and low-cost efforts can promote policy reform over the long term—by disseminating development ideas, training the next generation of leaders, and stimulating policy debate in civil society.

Development agencies have played an important role in disseminating information about what is good policy, both at the macroeconomic level and in individual sectors such as education, health, and pension reform (box 2.1). But good policy is not something subjectively decided by the World Bank; lessons emerge from the experiences of developing countries. Good management is, objectively, what has increased growth and reduced poverty in those countries.

Some key development policies (macroeconomic stability and openness) have become known as the "Washington consensus." This is an ironic designation because in the 1970s agencies such as the World Bank were not promoting these policies. In fact, the Bank was taken

---

Box 2.1   Reforming Pension Schemes

MANY DEVELOPING AND TRANSITION ECONOMIES have unsustainable public pension schemes—that is, pay as you go schemes that function as long as there are lots of workers and few retirees, but become unworkable when there are more retirees than workers. A World Bank report, *Averting the Old Age Crisis,* and its follow-up dissemination and technical assistance are a good example of how low-cost assistance can stimulate policy reform. Following the report, donors have helped many countries study the long-term fiscal and distributional consequences of their old-age security—Argentina, China, Hungary, Mexico, Poland, and Uruguay, for example. Officials involved in successful pension reform—in Chile, for instance—have been used to disseminate important messages. The thrust of technical assistance has been to help countries simulate the effect of their current pension systems and reform alternatives. In many cases these analyses have become a platform for public debate on pension reform and a way for the government to convince the public that reform is necessary.

with statist policies, such as those of Julius Nyerere in Tanzania. Through experience, however, the world has learned that this approach does not lead to sustained development. At the same time such policymakers as T.S. Chiang and T.C. Liu in Taiwan (China) were experimenting with policies that were not in fashion with the international development community.

It was only in the early 1980s that development agencies started to appreciate fully the value of sound macroeconomic management and began to promote trade liberalization and encourage closed economies to learn from the success of more open ones. It is hard to assess the impact of this dissemination of ideas. Sachs and Warner (1995) identify 35 countries that liberalized trade in the past 10 years. These countries almost certainly were influenced by past successes in other countries. Did development agencies play an important part in disseminating knowledge about successful policies? Likely, yes—but it cannot be proved one way or another.

Development assistance can also promote dissemination of knowledge about development by funding programs to send students abroad—to study economics, law, public administration, and so on. Returning students often play a key role in policy reform—either directly as government employees or officials or indirectly through work in domestic universities and the media. One famous example is the Berkeley group that designed Indonesia's reform in the late 1960s and early 1970s. Over the past 10 years many reforms in Latin America have been designed and implemented by ministers who studied economics abroad. In Botswana the U.S. Agency for International Development had a long-standing program that trained most government officials.

One study of the political economy of reform concluded that few generalizations could be made about successful developing country reform (Williamson 1994, p. 589). Of critical importance was a "coherent economic team." In most cases key members of economic teams in reforming economies have at least some overseas economics training, usually supported by donors or by nongovernmental organizations, such as the Ford Foundation.

Overseas training is not, however, a panacea for reform. Instead, where other domestic political factors have started a reform movement, welltrained economists and civil servants are crucial for its success. There are also many cases where people have been trained but not put to effective

Where domestic political factors have started a reform movement, well-trained economists and civil servants are crucial for its success.

use. A recent study of aid in Africa by the Overseas Development Council includes both successful and unsuccessful examples:

Master's level staff in government earn a fifth of what they could earn working for one of Nairobi's international management consulting firms.

"Governments find it difficult to retain qualified staff because of internal management problems and low wages in the public sector. At independence, civil service salaries were typically much higher than salaries in the private sector. . . . In the Tanzania and Kenya of 1970, for instance, a government worker earned 14 and 11–16 percent more, respectively, than a private sector employee with the same experience and education. By the late 1980s, however, reckless patronage practices, along with inflation and persistent fiscal crisis, had devastated individual salaries. In Tanzania, the number of civil servants had increased from 135,000 in 1970 to 302,000, but civil service salaries had lost 94 percent of their former purchasing power . . . . African governments found it difficult to retain competent staff, particularly at higher grades and technical levels. Thus, one study describes a CIDA-funded project in Kenya that trained 13 economists to master's level between 1985 and 1991; within a year, ten had found jobs outside of government and the other three, freshly returned from Canada, were looking for better paid positions in the private sector. The problem is simply that master's level staff in government earn a fifth of what they could earn working for one of Nairobi's international management consulting firms or the resident mission of a donor agency.

"The most able often leave: across Africa, civil servants have accepted better-paid jobs in the private sector or migrated out of the country. According to the United Nations, some 50,000 to 60,000 middle and high-level African managers left their country of origin between 1986 and 1990. Many went to work for the aid agencies themselves, lured by salaries often five to ten times higher than in the public service. In Kenya, for instance, a World Bank project hired eight Kenyans for a project it was financing in the Ministry of Agriculture, paying them between $3,000 and $6,000 a month compared with a total compensation package of approximately $250 available to a senior economist in the civil service.

"In a country like Botswana that avoided economic crisis, the presence of a virtuous cycle results in a very different dynamic. Regularly paid and given the means to perform their jobs, civil ser-

vants stay in their positions. It is not unusual for a permanent secretary to remain in the same position for more than ten years.
Although private sector wages have increased recently and some
employees have left the civil service, few have left the country. The
case study reports USAID's claim that all but three of the 1,300 or
so Botswanans who have received master's level training in the
United States since independence have returned to the country"
(van de Walle and Johnston 1996, p. 89–92).

Clearly, well-trained officials can be an important input to good policy (witness Botswana). If other factors conspire to maintain poor policies, however, trained officials are likely to leave the public sector (though
they may still make a big contribution to development). But they often
emigrate, in which case training will not have provided the intended benefits to the country.

Stimulating debate in civil society about policy is an intangible way
for development assistance to influence policy reform. This is not easy.
Leaders in countries with poor policies have interests in maintaining
those policies. Highly distorted trade regimes, exchange rates, and agricultural prices, for example, can lead to corruption and rent seeking
among favored groups. In such cases donors should look for space to
develop a dialogue with the middle civil service—usually more technocratic than political—and with elements of civil society.

In Ukraine, for example, during an era of poor policies, the World
Bank decided that lending would be counterproductive. It would post-
pone reforms even further, and other interventions were needed—for
example, public education for the government and civil society. The
media, reformers within government, parliamentarians, nongovernmental organizations, and the private sector were involved in major seminars,
nationwide town meetings, and a weekly, high-profile roundtable with
the media on key economic and institutional reform issues. One champion of this program was the governor of Ukraine's central bank, who
participated actively and remarked publicly that the most important
things that the World Bank did in early transition to help promote
reforms and development were to refrain from large-scale lending and
implement the public education program.

There are few hard research results to show that disseminating good
ideas, sending students abroad, or stimulating policy debates in civil society leads to developing country policy reform and better performance.

*Stimulating debate
in civil society about
policy is one way for
development assistance
to influence policy
reform.*

But case studies suggest that these factors are often important. Moreover, such activities are inexpensive.

It is not easy for outsiders to generate reform.

If Commitment, Money—If Not, Ideas

THERE IS NO VALUE IN PROVIDING LARGE AMOUNTS OF MONEY to a country with poor policies, even if it technically commits to the conditions of a reform program. Providing adjustment loans to governments not serious about reform has been a major recent problem of foreign aid.

For many low-income countries, initiating economic reform is crucial for future progress. But it is not easy for outsiders to generate reform. In countries with poor policies, donors should concentrate on activities that might support reform in the long run—overseas scholarships, dissemination of ideas about policy reform and development, and stimulation of debate in civil society. In most cases these are relatively low-cost measures, so there is no contradiction with the strong message that most finance should go to poor countries that have made substantial progress with policy reform.

Our review also found that adjustment lending is most effective if a government is strongly committed to reform. This raises a question, however: if reform programs must have strong domestic support to succeed, is there any point in having conditional lending? One study argues that there is still a useful role for policy-based lending, but that the way that it is managed must be reformed (Collier 1997). In the past donor agencies have tried to "buy reform" by offering assistance to governments that were not otherwise inclined to reform. This approach failed. Moreover, this use of conditionality undermines its potential value. Governments truly committed to reform may agree to a conditional loan that binds them to a policy and protects them from internal special interests. Such a conditional loan is a type of restraint that helps government resist the temptation to deviate from good policy in the pursuit of short-run interests.

Conditional loans can also be useful as signaling devices. Uncertainties about policy retard investment. Conditional loans can indicate to the private sector that government is serious about reform and the new policy regime is likely to persist. In good-policy countries, aid is associated with higher private investment; the combination of reform and foreign assistance can boost investor confidence. Collier points out that the way in which policy-based lending has been managed tends to undermine its usefulness as a restraint and signaling mechanism. These loans have not been useful as restraints (since funds have been disbursed regardless of whether reform has been carried out) and have not been good signals of the seriousness of reform (before 1990 one-third of adjustment loans failed).

The role of agencies such as the World Bank is not to arm-twist governments to do what they are reluctant to do. Nor is it true that if the World Bank works harder or puts more resources into an adjustment loan, a failed reformer can somehow be turned into a successful one. Instead, the role of international institutions should be to disseminate information that might influence public dialogue about policy reform—and to learn to read the signals about whether governments are serious or not. Mistakes are inevitable, but the success of adjustment loans should be closer to 85 percent than 67 percent. This target could be achieved by being more selective about the environments in which donors become involved in financing adjustment.

Collier argues further that for this approach to be effective, adjustment loans need to focus on fewer, but truly important measures. (In the Dollar-Svensson sample the mean number of conditions is 46, and the maximum 193.) For such loans to be effective as a restraint, there has to be clear agreement between government and donor agencies about what is important and the grounds for nondisbursement. To be effective as a signal, loans would have to have a high success rate (say, 85 percent). They would then be accurate signals to the private sector that the government receiving the loans is seriously committed to reform.

To be effective, adjustment loans need to focus on fewer, but truly important measures.

CHAPTER 3

Money Matters—In a Good Institutional Environment

ONEY MATTERS—BUT NOT IN THE WAY WE thought. Projects financed by foreign aid are often highly visible and important successes— roads and highways, schools and health clinics, irrigation infrastructure, power plants. But success can be assessed at two levels—at the micro or project level, which typically shows high rates of success or at the macro level of economywide growth and poverty reduction, where, as chapter 1 has shown, there is less visible success. If aid financing is fungible, the benefits of an aid-financed project are only loosely connected with the actual benefits of aid financing. Aid's true effect depends on the crucial (but difficult to assess) question: what would have happened in the absence of donor financing?

Most aid goes to projects to assist particular sectors (figure 3.1). Do these targeted resources reach these sectors? Or is foreign aid fungible? Specifically, if donors finance a $1 million project in education, does the recipient country spend more on education than if the donors had simply provided $1 million of budget support? The issue is not corruption, nor is it a question of administrative arrangements for aid flows. Instead, a person—or country—given resources "in kind" will rationally reallocate their other expenditures.

If aid is not fungible, evaluating the overall effect of aid is easy: it is simply the collective effect of individual projects. If primary education is important, more projects in this area should lead to overall improvements. If aid is typically fungible, however, managing and assessing the effect of aid is much more complicated. What you see is *not* what you get. Evaluating aid's effect requires not just examining what happened in the lifetime of a project, but judging what would have happened had there been no aid.

The first section of this chapter explores in detail what is meant by fungibility. We then look at the available evidence on several dimensions of fungibility. If a donor finances an investment for education, for instance, what confidence does it have that the resources:

■ Stick with the government rather than finance, say, tax reductions?
■ Finance investment rather than expanding consumption spending?
■ Finance education rather than some other sector?

Donors cannot be certain that resources actually go to the area favored by the project. So, we examine the implication of fungibility for evaluating projects.

One possibility is that in practice the actual effect of financing tied to projects is to raise government spending exactly as if general budgetary support were given. This implies that, even when donors are financing projects, an assessment of aid's effect as a financial transfer depends on a judgment of overall government spending—whether expenditures are allocated to activities likely to promote development and how effective the spending is. This involves assessing the rationale for government spending. Again, what you see is not necessarily what you get, as the key question is: what would have happened without government interventions?

What does fungibility mean for analyzing the allocation and efficiency of government spending and for managing and evaluating development assistance? In countries with sound policies, appropriate allocations of expenditures, and effective services, donors can provide large amounts of assistance as general budget support, knowing the resources will be well used. In cases where there is agreement about allocation but efficiency is low, aid projects and financing should be evaluated not just as money for a particular project but also for what they contribute to improving the overall efficacy of government expenditures (see chapter 4). Where donors and governments do not agree on the allocation of expenditures and spending is not likely to be effective, the best approach is to reduce funding and increase support for policy dialogue and institution building—until donors are convinced that their funds will contribute to development.

Most aid goes to projects—and most project aid goes to social, economic, and administrative infrastructure.

Figure 3.1 Distribution of Aid, by Type and Sector

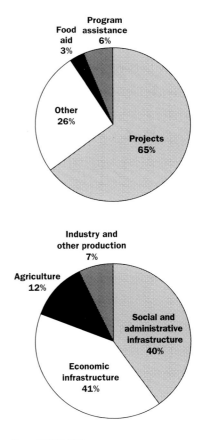

Source: OECD 1998.

Fungibility?

Fungibility is an issue only if the objectives of donors and recipients are different.

Figure 3.2 Full Fungibility

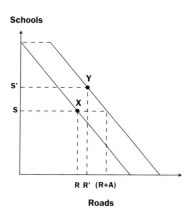

Schools

Source: Hypothetical illustration.

FIRST, A SHORT BUT INFORMATIVE DETOUR. MANY GOVERNMENT programs transfer income to individuals—income that is tied to specific purchases or that is transferred "in kind" rather than in cash. A prime example is a food stamp program that provides vouchers to be redeemed for the purchase of a limited list of food items. Even if the program is free of corruption (so that every food stamp dollar is redeemed for food), does such a program have a greater effect on people's food consumption than if they had been given cash?

Compare two views. The naive "what you see is what you get" view is that, if food stamps bought food, food consumption increased dollar for dollar. The "fungibility" view is that food stamp recipients are sophisticated and have their own objectives, in which case the recipient would reduce expenditures on food from their non–food stamp income dollar-for-dollar with increases in food stamp expenditures. So a dollar's worth of food stamps, even when spent on food, will increase food consumption by exactly the same amount as would have a dollar given in cash.

Which view is right? For food stamps there is solid evidence. Puerto Rico "cashed out" food stamps in 1982, and evidence suggests that this had little or no effect on food expenditures (Moffitt 1989). In the United States two randomized experiments of "cash out" found no effect on food expenditures in Alabama and only a small effect in San Diego (Fraker and others 1995). With food stamps the empirical evidence is overwhelming —that the naive view is wrong and the fungibility view is (almost exactly) right. But how does this relate to foreign aid?

A simple diagram helps illustrate three points about the fungibility of foreign aid (figure 3.2). Suppose that a government spends on only two goods, roads and schools, and in its budget it chooses to spend *R* on roads and *S* on schools (point X on the budget line). Now suppose that a donor is willing to make a grant of amount *A* to finance roads. If donor money is not at all fungible, this entire amount would be spent on roads. Thus the government would spend *R+A* on roads, and the same amount as before on schools (*S*). But if the money is completely fungible, the government's new budget is effectively the pre-grant budget plus *A* (as long as the government meets the condition of spending more than *A* on roads). In this example the government would then spend *R'* on roads (more than the pre-grant *R* and more than *A* but less than *R+A*) and *S'* on schools. This illustrates three points.

First, all of the aid (*A*), or its equivalent, is spent on roads in an administrative sense in all cases, but the effect of aid spent on roads on the *total* spending on roads could range anywhere from zero to the total amount *A*.

Second, full fungibility does not mean that none of the aid gets spent on roads, just that the effect on total road spending of providing amount *A* for roads is exactly the same as if the amount were provided as general budget support. The practical importance of fungibility depends on whether the donor and recipient have the same objectives. If the donor simply wishes to expand the budget available to the government but it is administratively convenient to provide funding for roads, then fungibility is unimportant. If, on the other hand, the donor has different preferences and really wanted the amount *A* to be spent on roads, then fungibility is a problem.

Third, fungibility requires that the amount of aid provided for roads is smaller than that which the government would have spent on roads from its own resources. Suppose that the government would have chosen to spend at point X on roads and schools and then receives road aid of amount A (figure 3.3). Then actual expenditures will increase to point Y, but had the transfer been untied, the government would have chosen point Z. Thus fungibility is less likely if the amount of aid is large relative to the government's budget (as in many aid-dependent economies) or if the item to which the financing is tied is specific and only a tiny fraction of the government budget (for example, project aid made available for an entirely new type of spending).

Most foreign aid goes to projects in which the donor finances either a single large investment (such as a highway) or, more often, a cluster of related investments (rural roads, urban housing, systems of irrigation canals, water supply for a number of villages, programs of school construction). Yet the fungibility of aid financing has been recognized as an issue from the beginning of large-scale aid.[1] The analytical possibility is not new, but what is new is the evidence on fungibility. Suppose that a donor provides $1 million to a government for an investment in a specific project in, say, education. The three relevant questions are:

- Does government spending rise by $1 million?
- Does government development spending rise by $1 million?
- Does education spending rise by $1 million?

Figure 3.3 Partial Fungibility

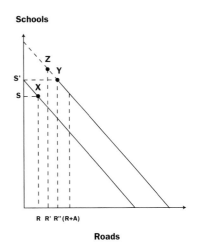

Source: Hypothetical illustration.

63

Does Aid Increase Government Spending?

Governments have several options when they receive aid. They can increase spending dollar for dollar. They can reduce taxes dollar for dollar. Or they can leave current spending and taxation unchanged and use the aid to reduce the deficit (equivalent to cutting future taxes)—or any mix of the three.

There is apparently a greater "flypaper" effect with concessional loans than with grants.

There is a large body of literature on the effect of transfers between one level of government and another in the same country—say, between the central government and provincial (or state) governments. The evidence is that money from higher-level to local governments tends to pass more into government spending and less into tax relief than a pure fungibility view would suggest. This tendency for nontax resources to "stick" to higher levels of government spending and not be passed on as tax relief is called the "flypaper" effect.

With foreign aid there is a wide range of estimates of the size of the flypaper effect. Two studies based on sizable samples of countries find that $1 in aid translates into much less than $1 in government spending. Feyzioglu, Swaroop, and Zhu (1997) looked at 38 countries and found that $1 in concessional loans (such as those from the International Development Association) leads to 63 cents in additional government spending (figure 3.4). For concessional loans and grants combined, the effect is only 33 cents. Thus there is apparently a greater flypaper effect with concessional loans than with grants. In a sample of 46 countries, Cashel-Cordo and Craig (1990) found that bilateral loans had no effect on government spending.

Studies based on smaller samples and individual countries find stronger flypaper effects. Feyzioglu, Swaroop, and Zhu (1997) use a subsample of 14 countries for which they had detailed data over time about government spending by sector (appendix 3). There was a complete flypaper effect: $1 of aid translated into roughly $1 of government spending (95 cents for bilateral loans and $1.24 for concessional loans). In a case study of Indonesia, Pack and Pack (1990) found that $1 in aid leads to $1.50 in additional government spending (figure 3.4). Thus, instead of providing tax relief by substituting for domestic resource mobilization, aid may increase taxation by "crowding in" government spending. This "crowding in" is possible if aid helps government mobilize other resources through improved tax collection or better access to commercial funds—or if aid relieves constraints that were limiting government spending.

Figure 3.4 A Dollar's Worth of Aid and Government Expenditure

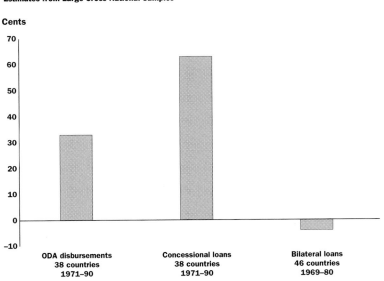

Estimates from Large Cross National Samples

Cents

Source: Feyzioglu, Swaroop, and Zhu 1998; Cashel-Cordo and Craig 1990.

In large samples, a dollar's worth of aid leads to significantly less than a dollar's worth of government expenditure . . .

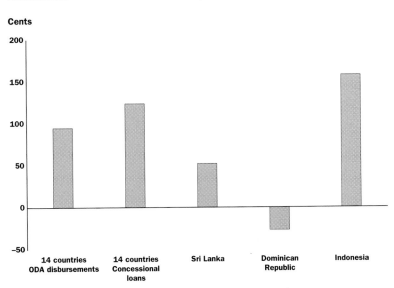

Estimates from Individual Countries and Small Samples

Cents

Source: Feyzioglu, Swaroop, and Zhu 1998; Pack and Pack 1990, 1993, 1996.

. . . but in individual countries strong "flypaper" effects are sometimes observed.

65

It is difficult to find the link between aid and development spending.

This supports the view that aid is largely fungible. Fungibility means that a government can use increased resources as it chooses—to increase spending, fund tax cuts, or reduce the fiscal deficit (reducing future taxes). Different societies will make different choices, so it will be possible to find examples (such as Indonesia) in which government spending rises hand-in-hand with aid. But this relationship is not seen uniformly in large samples of countries, which suggests that although there is some flypaper effect, it is not generally true that $1 in aid increases government spending by a full $1. Some goes to tax relief or deficit reduction.

Does Aid Increase Development Spending?

Donor financing and funding for projects is typically not structured to finance government spending in general. Instead, it is aimed at particular projects or specific expenditures, such as investment in infrastructure or social services. In developing country budgets these are usually captured in the distinction between "recurrent" and "development" expenditures.

Many developing countries have weak data on how government spending is split between development expenditures and other spending (administration, subsidies, defense, and so on). Thus it is difficult to find the link between aid and development spending in a large sample of countries. A general idea can be gained, however, by examining the relationship between aid and government consumption spending.

In their sample of 14 countries, Feyzioglu, Swaroop, and Zhu find that $1 in foreign aid typically results in 29 cents of public investment (figure 3.5). These, remember, were countries with a strong flypaper effect, so aid went dollar-for-dollar to government spending. It seems, though, that aid financed the government in general, not the development expenditures that donors typically target. In this sample 29 cents was the exact amount of a typical dollar of government spending from all sources (aid and non-aid) that goes into investment. Thus an aid dollar had exactly the same effect as one from any other source of government revenue.

The strong effect of aid (especially bilateral aid) on government consumption spending is seen in the same large sample of countries used in chapter 1 (figure 3.6). The strong association of more aid with higher government consumption spending (even after controlling for other determinants of government spending) suggests both a flypaper effect (that resources stuck) and fungibility (that allows aid provided for investment to finance consumption spending).

Figure 3.5 A Dollar's Worth of Aid and Government Investment ("Development") Expenditures

The typical aid dollar finances 29 cents of public investment . . .

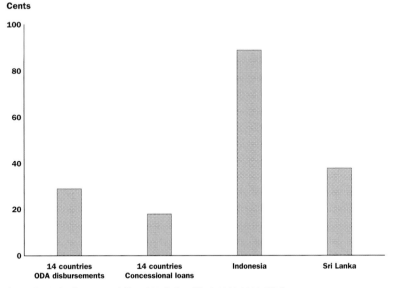

Cents

Source: Feyzioglu, Swaroop, and Zhu 1998; Pack and Pack 1990, 1993, 1996.

Figure 3.6 Bilateral Aid and Government Consumption

. . . most of the rest goes to government consumption.

Government consumption as a percentage of GDP

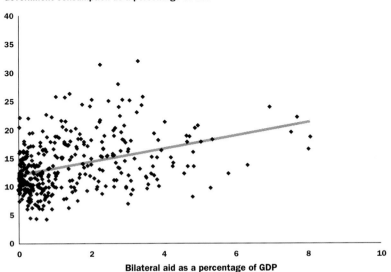

Bilateral aid as a percentage of GDP

Source: Calculated from the Burnside-Dollar data set.

67

Empirical studies of Indonesia and Sri Lanka also find that aid has a smaller effect on development spending than on total government spending, so that not all aid passes into investment. Again, the differences across countries are large. In Sri Lanka an additional aid dollar raised government spending by 52 cents. Of that, 38 cents was devoted to development spending and 14 cents to consumption spending. In Indonesia a dollar's worth of aid raised spending by $1.58, of which development expenditures accounted for 89 cents.

The evidence suggests that, even where aid goes mostly to government spending, the spending funded by aid is largely fungible between consumption and investment, regardless of whether the aid is administratively targeted to specific investment projects.

Does Project Aid Finance Particular Sectors?

Researchers have also tried to address sectoral fungibility—that is, does higher foreign assistance for a particular sector (for example, agriculture or education) raise spending for that sector? There are two ways to answer

A dollar's worth of aid to agriculture leads to less than a dollar's spending on agriculture.

Figure 3.7 A Dollar's Worth of Aid to Agriculture and Spending on Agriculture

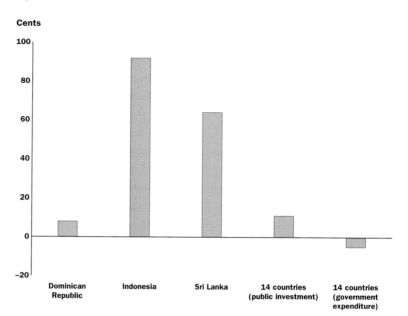

Source: Feyzioglu, Swaroop, and Zhu 1998; Pack and Pack 1990, 1993, 1996.

that question: by comparing spending over time within a country and comparing spending across countries. Whatever the method, the answer is the same: it varies. In some countries and sectors aid appears to be completely fungible across sectors, while in other countries and sectors the money seems to "stick."

Pack and Pack (1990) show that for every dollar increase in donor financing for Indonesian agriculture, expenditures in that sector increase by 92 cents. In contrast, a cross-sectional study of 14 countries finds that agricultural expenditures *decrease* by five cents for every $1 in aid given to agriculture (figure 3.7).

The net effect of an aid dollar on spending in a specific sector depends not only on the composition of the aid received, but also on how government responds to aid flows. Take education and health, and the results for a cross-sectional sample of 14 countries. The direct effect on education spending of a dollar in aid depends on the allocation of aid among sectors: 8.7 cents of every aid dollar are allocated to education and health. With sectoral fungibility, however, that is not the whole picture, which depends on whether aid for education leads to a reduction in what the government otherwise would have spent on school programs, and whether aid for other sectors causes the government to spend more on education. In the estimates from the 14 countries, the net effect of a dollar's worth of aid is to reduce education and health expenditures by 6.5 cents, even though on average 8.7 cents was devoted to education and health (figure 3.8).

The effect varies enormously by country. In Sri Lanka 5.9 cents of an aid dollar go to education and health, but the estimated net effect is to *reduce* spending by 1.9 cents. Indonesia receives a similar proportion devoted to education and health, 7.2 cents, but the effect is to *increase* spending by 18.9 cents; clearly money earmarked for other sectors was reallocated to education and health. The important point is that government commitment to particular sectors is more important than targeting aid.

These statistics do not tell the whole story of consequences. It may be that the observed changes in public expenditures are exactly what donors wanted anyway. The donor objective, for example, may not be to increase total education spending, but to increase spending on primary education while reducing spending on higher education. But a shift in the allocation of spending requires agreement between donors and the government based on analysis and dialogue.

Government commitment to particular sectors is more important than targeting aid.

A dollar's worth of aid to education may lead to little (or no) additional spending on education.

Figure 3.8 A Dollar's Worth of Aid to Health and Education and Spending on Health and Education

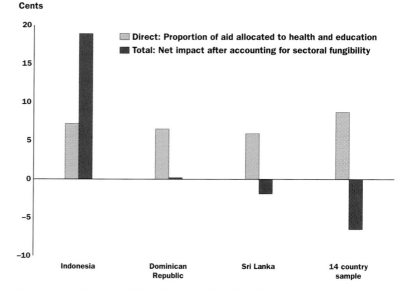

Source: Feyzioglu, Swaroop, and Zhu 1998; Pack and Pack 1990, 1993, 1996.

Budgetary Mechanics of Fungibility

The magnitude of fungibility depends on a country's budgetary structures, the degree to which governments are able to manage their finances, and the extent of donor involvement.

In India's complicated federal fiscal system of transfers between the central government and individual states, for instance, the budgetary system was designed so that the donor financing coming through the central government to projects in specific states would not affect either the projects chosen or the total transfers received by the states. This made fungibility explicit. The Indian budgetary system was designed so that projects were chosen to be part of the public sector investment plan or not, and then financing was obtained for those projects. The evidence from an empirical study suggests that aid to the Indian central government was fully fungible, both between development and nondevelopment spending and across sectors (Jha and Swaroop 1997). Other countries, such as Mexico, have incorporated mechanisms into their budgetary system to create fungibility: the goal of their system is to ensure that budget allocations are not to be affected by the availability of finance.

The Indian system also determined the amount of investment financing from the central government to each state. In the past, if states received a larger amount of support from donors, their transfer for development spending on capital account from the central government was correspondingly reduced (Jha and Swaroop 1997).

One major weakness of aid in Africa is the lack of strong budgetary control by either government or society over public investment. A case study in Ghana, Malawi, and Uganda revealed that controls were too weak to accomplish any of the three main objectives of budgetary systems: developing aggregate budget discipline, imposing strategic priorities, and encouraging technical efficiency (Campos and Pradhan 1996). The big problem is that budgets are often ad hoc—that is, realized expenditures differ enormously from budgets, and there is a disconnect between the recurrent budget and the development budget. Moreover, donor financing, particularly through projects, is a large component of investment and total expenditures. For instance, donor project financing accounted for 71 percent of capital expenditures in Ghana and 87 percent in Uganda (table 3.1).

Weak systems of budgetary planning, control, and management, combined with large donor contributions, often cause "the bulk of the Public Investment Program to be determined by donor-driven priorities, thereby fragmenting and undermining the priority setting process within the countries" (Campos and Pradhan 1996, p. 29). Lack of government control over project selection and the budgeting process was one of the key problems in African aid identified in a recent study by the Overseas Development Council and implemented jointly with African researchers (van de Walle and Johnston 1996). Their case studies of seven countries found that donors often drove project selection and most projects had little recipient input. For example, in Senegal only 170 of 316 projects in

Realized expenditures differ enormously from budgets.

Table 3.1 Donor Financing of Investment Budgets in Two African Countries (percent)

	Ghana	*Uganda*
Project financing/capital expenditures	71	87
Project financing/total expenditures	27	43
All donor financing/total expenditures	32	67

Source: Campos and Pradhan 1996.

the public investment plan had been assessed using the appropriate internal procedures. Donor control likely meant that aid would be less fungible, but it raised other problems—such as a lack of government ownership and commitments to recurrent finance for projects.

Project Assessment with Fungible Money

These differences in fungibility across countries mean that it is pretty certain that what you see is *not* what you get. Moreover, it is difficult to know either before or after donors provide finance the extent of fungibility, and so exactly what was financed. But if money is fungible, evaluating donor-financed projects is beside the point, as their effect is not the same as that of donor financing. To take a hypothetical example: suppose there were 11 discrete projects, each of which cost $10 million. Suppose, also, that the economic returns on them ran from 100 percent (for project A), to 90 percent (project B), and so on down to 0 percent (project K). Suppose, finally, the country will invest $50 million from its own resources, while a donor provides $10 million—in total, enough to finance six projects. There are several possibilities (table 3.2).

Table 3.2 Evaluating the Effect of Projects with Fungibility

	Projects undertaken	Apparent effect of aid-financed project		Actual effect of aid financing	
		Project	Return	Project	Return
Base case	ABCDE				
Donor finances A, the highest-return project, freed resources finance F, the marginal project	ABCDE, F	A	100 percent	F	40 percent
Donor finances marginal project chosen by the government	ABCDE, F	F	40 percent	F	40 percent
Donor finances A, the highest-return project, and freed resources finance K, a low-return project	ABCDE, K	A	100 percent	K	0 percent
Donor finances A, the highest-return project, and freed resources finance consumption spending, or reduce taxes	ABCDE	A	100 percent	None	Unknown, could be large or small

Note: Based on an entirely hypothetical example in which there is a set of possible projects (each costing $10 million) with different economic rates of return—and in the absence of aid financing, the government chooses to implement five projects.
Source: Hypothetical illustration.

First, the government agrees that the donor will finance the highest-return project (A). Thus the apparent rate of return is 100 percent: that is, when the donor assesses the benefits it will find that its aid has been hugely successful. What really matters in evaluating the effect of aid, however, is what the government does with the resources it otherwise would have devoted to the project. It could do the next best project not yet financed, which would be F (with a return of 40 percent), since it is already committed to B,C,D, and E. Or the government could choose to do a white elephant project (K) with political payoffs but with a return to the economy of zero. It could also choose to reallocate the resources from investment to consumption. What is the return on additional consumption expenditures, high or low? Often consumption spending, such as that on recurrent inputs or operations and maintenance, is not financed by donors but has enormously high returns in keeping existing investments productive. So a shift from investment to consumption could have a huge return, say, 200 percent. Alternatively, the consumption could be the conspicuous consumption of the elite and have zero return. Or the aid could have financed tax relief, which as a "project" may have very high returns if it reduces distortionary taxes.

Delivering aid through projects has several advantages for donors. There are administrative advantages to organizing tasks into discrete, manageable units. Investment projects fit well with the notion that increasing investment is the key to development. And by financing particular items (family planning, education, and so on), projects appeal to single-interest coalitions in donor countries supporting foreign aid.

But while the project approach has some advantages for donors, it does not ensure that aid is put to good use. Nor does it facilitate the evaluation of aid effectiveness. If, say, aid finances a road project with a 20 percent rate of return, this information tells us next to nothing about aid effectiveness. Does fungibility imply that projects are irrelevant and should be abandoned as a way of organizing and delivering aid, in favor of broader financing mechanisms? Not at all. Project financing can be used to convey other value added. In many cases the project's value added was never intended to be the investment itself. Donors often are not trying to influence project selection or directly alter the sectoral composition of spending but are using projects as a vehicle for technology transfer or to build institutional capacity or reform sectoral policies.

Taking the road example, donor involvement may mean that those institutions responsible for roads are improved—or road policies are

While the project approach has some advantages for donors, it does not ensure that aid is put to good use.

changed for the better. Projects are a cauldron of money and ideas. Since the money does not necessarily stick with the sector, the design and evaluation of projects should focus on the contribution of ideas to altering sector institutions and policies (see chapter 4).

Donors are, more or less, financing whatever the government chooses to do.

Public Spending—Quality not Quantity

THE SAFEST ASSUMPTION FOR DONORS IS THAT THEY ARE, MORE or less, financing whatever the government chooses to do. Since donors are financing government in general, they need to consider all public expenditures, in terms of both allocation and efficiency, when deciding the appropriate level and method of aid. So donors must each decide, what makes for an effective public spending program?

Equity and Efficiency

Governments ought to be doing things where there is a convincing rationale for public involvement. Twenty or so years ago, donors willingly financed almost anything in which the government chose to try its hand—textile plants, shoe factories, steel mills, and all sorts of manufacturing. Not only were developing world parastatals financed through donor credits and loans; many government corporations were created because donor financing was available. There has been a clear shift in thinking about the value of government investments in shoe making or textile weaving. Today few people would dispute that these activities can just as easily (and with greater effect) be undertaken by the private sector. In general, the rationale for government intervention is to improve equity and efficiency. But government action that achieves these improvements proves difficult in practice.

Equity. Many government expenditures—even those traditionally justified by their improvements in equity—are not well targeted toward poverty alleviation. For instance, an assessment in Brazil found that social insurance payments in 1980 reached only better-off formal sector workers, so the richest 20 percent of workers received 12 times the benefits that went to the poorest 20 percent. In education, too, equity implications differ widely between primary and tertiary education, for instance. A study in Indonesia found that the richest fifth of households received only 60 percent of the benefits per person from public spending on primary education as the poorest fifth. Since children in richer households were more likely to remain in school, however, the higher the level of schooling, the greater the benefit to richer households. By senior secondary school, the richest fifth received 17 times the benefits of the poorest fifth (van de Walle 1995).

Efficiency. Justifying government actions to increase efficiency is also not always simple. The existence of market failures must be taken into account. But so, too, must their magnitude, particularly when compared with the likely "government failure" in implementing a proposed remedy. The notion that since market failures were pervasive, they were complete and therefore demanded government action, has been replaced by a nuanced view—that both market failures and government failures are pervasive, but not complete. So, although working from common principles, a country-by-country assessment is needed to determine the magnitude of market failure and the depth of government capacity (World Bank 1997b).

Nevertheless, the principle of efficiency often leads to clear recommendations. For instance, governments, sometimes supported by donor financing, have devoted substantial resources to manufacturing and trade that markets could have provided equally well and for which there was no underlying efficiency rationale. Moreover, governments have often used broad-based subsidies that lack rationale in either equity or efficiency—such as large-scale subsidies to agricultural products or fuels used mainly by richer consumers, which impose an explicit or implicit tax on poorer agricultural producers.

Quality and Quantity

The quality of government expenditures is typically more important than the quantity. While there is evidence about what kinds of public sector outputs are crucial to growth and poverty reduction (basic education and infrastructure, for instance), there is often little or no evidence that increasing public spending would have an impact on these objectives. Just as the effect of aid differs across countries, so too does the effect of increased public spending on improving outcomes. Cross-national and sectoral evidence, as well as individual cases, suggests that inputs like money are often not the most important issue for public sector outputs.

The empirical growth literature finds that government consumption has no positive effect on growth. Some studies find a negative effect, others

The quality of government expenditures is typically more important than the quantity.

The quantity of public spending on health bears little relationship to lower mortality.

Figure 3.9 Public Spending on Health as a Percentage of GDP and Health Outcomes

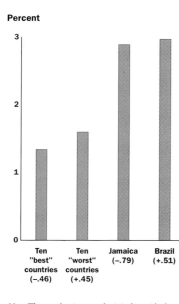

Note: The number in parenthesis is the residual from a regression of the natural log of under-5 mortality on GDP per capita and other socio-economic determinants of mortality.
Source: Filmer and Prichett 1997.

zero. The finding that aid largely finances government consumption, which has no positive effect on growth, again helps explain why aid is not fueling growth in many developing countries.

One study used data on economic growth and the allocation of government budgets for 43 developing countries to show that there was no relationship between economic growth and public capital spending (Devarajan, Swaroop, and Zou 1996). The authors found that increasing by one percent the share of public spending devoted to capital (versus current) spending would reduce economic growth by half a percentage point each year. Another study, using a specially created dataset on public investments, found that the share of GDP devoted to public investment had no association with economic growth, after controlling for a standard set of determinants of growth (Easterly and Rebelo 1993). So while one intended purpose of aid might be to increase public investment, the quantity of investment alone bears little relationship to economic growth. Examining the effect of the magnitude of public investment across countries shows that differences in the efficiency with which governments invest is as important in explaining growth as the amount they spend on investment (Pritchett 1996).

The data are similarly agnostic about the relationship between sectoral expenditures and economic growth. Devarajan, Swaroop, and Zou find no association between growth and the share of public spending devoted to education or health. Moreover, they find that both education and health spending per capita are consistently negatively related to growth. Easterly and Rebelo also find that the share of GDP going to public investment in education and health is unrelated to economic growth. There is little evidence from cross-country comparisons that more spending on public investment, or even reallocation across sectors, would automatically translate into better growth outcomes.

This finding is consistent with estimates of public spending efficiency for three major sectors: health, education, and infrastructure. Comparisons across countries suggest that public spending has some (small) effect on health. Ranking countries by the difference between actual child mortality and the level expected for their economic and social determinants of health, the 10 countries with the best performance in health typically spend 1.3 percent of GDP on health—and child mortality is 40 percent lower than would be expected (figure 3.9). The worst 10 have child mortality roughly 40 percent higher than expected, but actually devote a larger share of GDP to public spending on health than the 10 best (Filmer and Pritchett 1997).

In explaining any measure of mortality (infant, child) or life expectancy, regression analysis finds little or no correlation between public spending and health status (Musgrove 1996).

Likewise, in education there is little evidence that higher spending means higher quality schooling. Using assessments of educational performance in math and science based on internationally comparable examinations, one study found that both total and recurrent spending on education as a fraction of GDP was negatively related to test score achievements (Hanushek and Kim 1995). While most agree that a rapid expansion of skills was key to the pre-1997 success of the fast-growing East Asian economies, these countries are not distinguished by the extent of the resources devoted to education during its takeoff and after (public spending on education accounted for about 3 percent of GDP in the Republic of Korea) or by physical inputs such as the pupil-teacher ratio, which in 1985 was 38 in Korea, 31 in the Philippines, and 32 in Sri Lanka (Tan and Mingat 1992).

In infrastructure there are similar differences in cost and performance across countries (World Bank 1994). While the flow of infrastructure services is important for economic growth, it is harder to show that infrastructure expenditures (or even stocks) are important (Hulten 1996).

It will come as no surprise to anyone with experience in developing countries that comparisons show little connection between spending and outcomes. This does not mean, however, that spending cannot influence outcomes. The actual effect of spending in almost every area of endeavor—from infrastructure to education—has been much less than the potential.

When the *what* and the *how well* come together and governments do the *right* things *well,* the results can be amazing. An obvious example is the educational accomplishments in East Asia, where countries such as Korea have gone from widespread illiteracy to educational quality that rivals (and surpasses) that of much richer countries. There are similar examples in health, where the mobilization of public health efforts to attack problems of communicable diseases, diseases carried by pests, and water-borne diseases led to a revolution in health status. Sri Lanka and the state of Kerala in India have life expectancies far exceeding that predicted by their income and education. When the state of Ceara in Brazil was able to mobilize and energize government workers in the health sector, it achieved enormous reductions in infant mortality in a few years.

When the emphasis is on what government should do, and particularly how much it should spend, aid becomes a means to support spending, as

The actual effect of spending in almost every area of endeavor—from infrastructure to education—has been much less than the potential.

if spending were the end in itself. Thus aid flows independently of how effectively spending promotes poverty reduction. In many cases, even when donor resources increased investment in the right areas, it did not promote development. Thus it is not just what governments do, but how they do it and how well.

Donors must form an opinion on the allocation and effectiveness of a country's public spending.

What Should Donors Do?

WHAT ARE THE IMPLICATIONS OF FUNGIBILITY AND OF DIF-ferences in the quality of public spending for the way donors do business? Many discussions of aid policy concentrate on what donors ought to be financing: girls' education or rural feeder roads, agricultural extension or family planning clinics, power plants or vaccination campaigns. But if money is fungible among sectors (and it often is), then from the narrow view of expanding expenditures it simply does not matter what donors finance. Most development practitioners recognize fungibility, however, and have moved to a broader concept of the effect of donor financing: it is more than just an attempt to expand capital. This raises the question of how donors allocate effort and available resources to best assist each country. As with country-level policies, we return to two themes in choosing the magnitude and mode of assistance: timing and selectivity, and the role of money and ideas.

Form a View . . .

To pursue an effective development strategy, donors must form an opinion on the allocation and effectiveness of a country's public spending. Donors can help only if they know what a country's needs are. In the past decade public expenditure analysis has emerged as a useful tool to assess the value of government spending in different areas. Reviews of public expenditures have focused on how well budgets meet the three criteria of budgeting: fiscal discipline, priorities across sectors, and technical efficiency.

Donors need to be able to form a judgment on how well government spending is working along each of the three criteria. These reviews led to the elimination of many "white elephants." Scrutinizing (and often cutting) large planned investments that would later generate budget commitments was one fruitful result of public expenditure analysis.

Public spending analysis has also brought to the fore attention on issues within sectors—across subsectors and across functional categories. When countries are faced with fiscal adjustment, two common tendencies are across-the-board cuts in budget items and cuts in everything but payroll—approaches that are inefficient. Analysis has also been effective in bringing into focus subsectoral priorities—say, preserving primary education, less so tertiary, from budget cuts.

The first generation of public expenditure analyses did not go far enough. The analyses generally did not use a framework for spending that established justification for public expenditures or broad guidance about the appropriate composition of spending across sectors (Swaroop 1997). A review of 113 World Bank public expenditure reviews found that few even looked at the role of the state and public-private boundaries (McCarthy 1995). Moreover, very few reviews went beyond expenditures and linked them to specific outputs.

One painful lesson of experience is that government and community ownership of projects is crucial.

. . . and Use the View

Once donors have formed a view on the allocation and efficiency of public spending, what then? One common donor reaction to the fungibility of money is to try to avoid it by imposing additional conditions on aid financing beyond one project to ensure the additionality of resources at the sectoral level. Bad idea.

One way to ensure additionality is for donors to finance only items or projects that governments are not financing. Common sense tells us, however, that this reasoning is flawed. It would mean that donors finance only what countries and governments do not want to do. And government would have little or no commitment to implementing or, much less, maintaining projects once donors depart. Some governments (purposely or by default) have given donors free rein to do whatever they feel like. Money for such projects would almost certainly be "additional," but with equal certainty the projects themselves would be pointless, except in those rare cases that the project itself creates commitment. Far better that both recipients and donors be strongly committed to the sustainability of projects. But this is precisely when money will be fungible.

One painful lesson of experience is that government and community ownership of projects is crucial. Trying to make financing additional,

Donors should take it for granted that their financing is fungible because that is reality.

however, implies that there is a disagreement between donors and government about the allocation of expenditures but that donors have enough clout to ensure that governments will follow their recommendations on the overall allocation of spending. This is practically impossible. It is not just a question of saying that if a donor provides an additional $1 million that spending on the activity financed must increase by $1 million because spending might have increased by that amount in the absence of the extra aid. To ensure additionality, donors would have to make governments promise that they are spending $1 million more than they would have had they not received the aid. But they would say that in any case, wouldn't they?

In fact, donors should take it for granted that their financing is fungible because that is reality. This, in turn, requires rethinking how aid is delivered. Efficient delivery in different countries depends on the nature of public spending and the efficiency of the public sector. One measure of public sector efficiency is the index of economic management. And an earlier recommendation was that of two equally poor countries, well-managed countries should receive more finance than poorly managed ones (see chapter 1).

In a country with sound public expenditure management, a larger portion of aid can be in the form of general budget support. This recognizes the reality of fungibility and economizes on the administrative costs of aid. These are important—a typical World Bank project runs about $1 million in administrative costs. If a project is merely replicating what the country already does relatively well (building another power plant in a well-managed system), there is little value added from administrative costs. Providing general budget support would free these staff and donor resources for other, higher-value added activities.

Problems with public expenditure management are usually one of two types: inefficiency in allocation of resources across activities or inefficiency in the use of allocated resources.

Composition of Spending. Consider first a country that does things reasonably well, but continues to spend on many things that are inefficient because the private market could do these things just as well or the social returns are simply too low. Suppose that a country insists on putting large amounts of public finance into higher education. Donors traditionally want to fund primary education to expand its relative share of the budget. But with fungibility this approach is not rational. Possibly a better approach is "time slice" financing of the education budget.

Developed specifically for this purpose are such instruments as the Sector Investment Program. Donors and recipient governments reach a broad agreement on the goals for the sector—and develop projects and programs to achieve these goals. Donors then finance particular projects within the agreed program or provide general support to the sector budget. Periodic reviews of the Sector Investment Program provide a forum where donors and recipient governments can frankly exchange views on the overall sector spending program. Donors can use this policy dialogue to improve the allocation of expenditures. Another mechanism some have tried is a Medium-term Expenditure Framework that tries to produce a strategic direction for government. Case studies of Ghana and Uganda, however, have found these less successful than hoped. In Ghana, some expenditures are designated as core. Pressures to include more items in the core led to the creation of a "supercore," which was just as pressured. Both concepts were abolished in 1990. One cannot expect miracles, however, and some early experiences with these innovations are showing natural implementation difficulties.

While it is useful to have an open dialogue, it is unrealistic to expect complete consensus on the important activities for government to undertake. There are still wide divisions of opinion about the right role for government between and within donor and recipient countries. Some people believe that governments should subsidize tertiary schooling. Others do not. Some believe that governments should play a strong role in allocating credit. No, say others. The government should provide electricity, say some. Many disagree. These are not just disagreements about the extent and nature of market failure but about values, like the extent to which governments should take redistributive action. Technocratic advice will not be sufficient to resolve most disputes about allocations across sectors or within sectors across categories of spending. In 1990 Sweden spent three times Japan's 11.5 percent of GDP on social transfers (Lindert 1994). Given the enormous differences among donor countries in the allocation of spending and of private and public responsibilities, it is hard to believe that a sharp consensus will emerge from the democratic process even among donors, much less between donors and recipient governments.

Effectiveness of Spending. Suppose now that an aid recipient has spending allocations that donors broadly support, but is inefficient in delivering services. If a country has carried out macroeconomic reforms, it should be getting a significant amount of aid. Macroeconomic reform is not technically difficult, but developing an efficient public sector is more challenging.

There are still wide divisions of opinion about the right role for government between and within donor and recipient countries.

In this case donors should largely stick with the project approach. The main objective of projects now is not to increase funding for a particular activity, but to help change the institutions and policies at the micro level that affect service delivery. An assessment of public sector efficiency is needed to make an informed decision about how to deliver aid. Once countries have carried out macroeconomic reforms, those with efficient public sectors can receive budget support, while those with inefficient public sectors would get relatively less money and more ideas.

Where a country has both a severely distorted allocation of expenditures and an inefficient public sector, institutions and policies will be poor and finance will be of little value. The traditional donor response has, nevertheless, been to try to find something useful to finance. Fungibility helps explain why large amounts of aid have had no lasting effect in these highly distorted environments. There is no alternative to patience. But there are a variety of ways that donors can, without large flows, support the creation of an environment for productive public expenditures, the subject of chapter 4.

Note

1. The World Bank's first Chief Economist, Paul Rodenstein-Rodan, emphasized in the 1950s that even when financing was tied to projects, money often remained fungible. Assessments of aid as early as the 1960s raised the issue of fungibility (Little and Clifford 1965).

CHAPTER 4

Aid Can Be the Midwife of Good Institutions

A S THE WORLD'S ECONOMIES MOVE INEXORABLY TO embrace market-friendly policies, public sectors are reorienting themselves and downsizing. "Less is better," has been the cry. But could this response go too far? In many crucial areas there are essential public responsibilities—in developing human, institutional, and physical infrastructure—that government must continue to fulfill. In these areas, less is not necessarily better, but "better is better."

One key to development is that government must do well those things that government must do. Since aid (both money and ideas) mostly supports the public sector, one pressing question is: How can development assistance be designed so that it helps governments carry out better the activities essential to increasing growth and reducing poverty? Another is: How can aid combine financial support with help to create local knowledge so that governments can improve the quality and effectiveness of public services?

Creating knowledge does not mean that donor agencies (or the experts they hire) have chunks of technical or engineering information that they simply transmit to aid recipients. In the public sector, development knowledge is needed to design and effectively run the institutions responsible for public services: primary schools in El Salvador, water supply in Guinea, road maintenance in Tanzania, or utility regulation in Argentina. This is not knowledge that exists somewhere and can be packed in a suitcase and carried to developing countries. To be effective, this is knowledge that must be created locally and internalized. Existing principles must always be adapted to new or local circumstances (or both), and developing country governments and citizens must take

How can development assistance be designed so that it helps governments carry out better the activities essential to increasing growth and reducing poverty?

83

Before choosing instruments, aid donors first need to be clear about goals.

the lead in creating this new knowledge. Development agencies can, however, bring unique value added to the table.

A consistent focus on improving the quality of the public sector implies a radical shift in the way aid business is done—in the choice of instruments, how those instruments are used and evaluated, and how donors relate to governments and civil society.

Before choosing instruments, aid donors first need to be clear about goals. The role of aid varies depending on country circumstances; the mix of financial and nonfinancial development assistance must be tailored to specific needs. In the few poor countries where the public sector is already effective, the task of foreign aid is straightforward: simply financing the expansion of public services is likely to be both successful and beneficial. In most developing countries, however, governments are not effective at providing public services, and financing more of the same is unlikely to be successful or beneficial. In these cases foreign assistance should focus on increasing the effectiveness of core public services. This requires the right mix of finance and ideas to produce the greatest value added. Money does not usually matter most. Aid agencies must look beyond providing finance to supporting the creation of knowledge.

A combination of policy dialogue and financing is more likely to increase aid effectiveness than a narrow focus on successful implementation of aid-financed projects. At times, donors have hindered the creation of effective public sectors because they saw end runs around local institutions as the easiest way to achieve project success. Donors need to convince countries of the value of better policies and institutions rather than cocoon "their" projects from the worst consequences of those policies.

Better Public Provision

PROVIDING PUBLIC SERVICES EFFECTIVELY AND EFFICIENTLY requires that all stakeholders—governments, providers (whether public employees or private), and citizens—have reasonable incentives. These incentives can be manifold: from making governments responsive to citizens to ensuring the right structure of civil service pay, to designing concession contracts that fit country and sector circumstances.

Accountability

No longer can governments be monopoly providers of services (education, health, roads, irrigation, water, and so on) with no accountability to citizens (directly or indirectly) for their performance. In recent years donors have moved to support accountability and governance as well as innovations that support greater community "voice"and involvement. In a range of sectors these reforms carry different names and take different forms but reflect the same impetus—rural water supply ("participation"), irrigation systems ("water user associations"), schools ("decentralization" and "school autonomy"), transport ("road management boards"), health ("community associations"), and environmental management ("community forestry").

Donor finance can affect accountability and the quality of public services for good or ill. In the irrigation sector examples abound of how an emphasis by governments and donors on quantitative (or investment) targets and modern technologies led to the exclusion of the intended beneficiaries from planning, design, and implementation. Sometimes that exclusion can lead to almost absurd results. One major donor-financed irrigation system in Nepal was designed by technical staff on the assumption that the area was unirrigated (Ostrom 1996). A fortuitous delay in the project provided the time to discover that, in fact, there were 85 fully functioning farmer-managed irrigation systems. Beneficiary involvement would have saved red faces. Another Nepalese irrigation scheme actually lowered agricultural productivity by undermining preexisting arrangements among farmers (Hilton 1990, 1992).

A recurring problem with irrigation projects has been inadequate revenues for operations and maintenance. Merely raising water fees does not solve the problem unless providers are accountable and the necessary revenues are devoted to maintenance. Even when revenues are available for maintenance, the organizational structure of the provider can be a problem. One study compares irrigation systems in India and the Republic of Korea (Wade 1995). While the two systems are similar, the different design of their irrigation departments (responsible for delivering water) leads to enormous differences in performance. In India the department is a centralized bureaucracy that relies on general treasury revenues for finance; in Korea irrigation officials are local and in constant contact with farmers.

Such problems are not unique to irrigation, but plague service delivery in many other sectors—water supply, health care, education, road maintenance—due partly to the way aid projects have been structured. The

Donor finance can affect accountability and the quality of public services for good or ill.

emphasis on increasing the quantity of financial aid as the answer to increasing growth has led agencies to targets that centered on the size and speed of disbursements and a technocratic approach to the design of investments. Even when all parties know better, "moving the money" can easily and quickly become the paramount institutional objective (Tendler 1975). With that kind of thinking, agencies opt for large projects rather than small ones and prefer to deal directly with centralized agencies on efficiency grounds (box 4.1). Doing so makes accounting and administration easier. In many cases donor investment projects—with fixed schedules and budgets—have left no room for beneficiary involvement. In some cases this led to "approval cultures" in aid agencies, where success was judged by the volume of disbursements (World Bank 1992).

Reviews of the Danish donor agency's 30-year experience in Tanzania's rural water sector found that the same problems (lack of maintenance, low community interest) occurred repeatedly, yet only modest changes were made in project design. The agency's procedures were dictated by a need to implement projects rather than to create supplies of water that met the needs of beneficiaries. A review of the World Bank's irrigation experience suggests that although the benefits of user participation are large, "irrigation professionals are wary of such participation, because they know it will lengthen the implementation period" (Jones 1995, p. 141).

Some measure of the importance of beneficiary participation in project success can be gleaned from an evaluation of 121 rural water supply projects financed by donors and nongovernmental organizations in 49 countries (Narayan 1995; Isham, Narayan, and Pritchett 1995). As

Box 4.1   Aid and Centralization

"STRENGTHENING THE ROLE OF LOCAL GOVERNMENTS, especially in the delivery of public services—for example, health, social welfare, agricultural extension, and rural infrastructure provision, all of which have all been devolved in the Philippines—is intuitively desirable. But in practice decentralization has led to problems in the formulation of donor projects. The problem does not arise so much in the case of grant assistance as in loan-funded projects, where the question of loan conduiting can become a stumbling block. Donor agencies are not normally prepared to lend directly to local governments without a guarantee from the national government. But providing such a guarantee runs counter to the principle of devolving responsibility to the local government. In the absence of satisfactory loan conduiting mechanisms for local governments, national government agencies tend to formulate projects that involve devolved functions, undermining the devolution process" (Habito, in OECF/World Bank 1998, p. 21).

shown in the overview among projects with a high level of participation, 68 percent were highly successful. But of those projects in which there was little beneficiary involvement, only 12 percent were highly effective. Another important finding was that not only was participation crucial to success, but also that it could be encouraged, or discouraged, through project design and government action. Implementing agencies which actively sought to involve intended beneficiaries had 62 percent of their projects achieve success (figure 4.1). In contrast, government agencies that did not actively seek beneficiary involvement ended up with less effective projects and only 10 percent were highly successful.

Another study found that investment projects have been more effective in countries where citizens enjoy civil liberties (Isham, Kaufmann, and Pritchett 1997). This is not a measure of political democracy but of people's freedom to express their views (free press, freedom of association and assembly, freedom to petition governments). Civil liberties matter even among projects assessed on the economic rate of return—projects that might be thought to be entirely technocratic matters for engineers and economists and insulated from popular pressures (appendix 4). Indeed, the probability of a project failing (those with *ex post* economic returns below a cutoff of 10 percent) is 50 percent higher in countries with fewer civil liberties (figure 4.2).

Donors are moving to encourage beneficiary involvement and local ownership. To that end, they have embarked on numerous innovations, including social investment funds. These funds do not specify a particular set of projects by sector (a road project, say, or new schools in particular villages). Instead, they specify processes whereby communities can apply for funds for any project they wish to undertake, subject to reasonable conditions on cost, need, sustainability, community contribution, and so on. Such funds have been created in more than 20 countries, and a preliminary evaluation suggests that they have been reasonably successful. They force changes on donor agencies from project to process: the fund must specify a process for funding projects and assess the likelihood that this process will produce projects that generate sustained benefits. But the evaluation found that even social funds maintain features that are an end run around institutional weaknesses and hence are only a temporary solution.

Donors are also becoming more flexible about allowing midstream adjustments in projects and encouraging "structured learning" so that development objectives are met. An example is the World Bank's support to Brazil's PROSANEAR sanitation project. Sponsored in part by Caixa

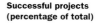

When agencies sought participation as a goal, 62 percent of projects were successful—when not, only 10 percent.

Figure 4.1 Participation and Project Success

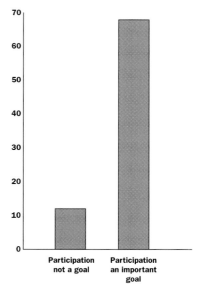

Successful projects
(percentage of total)

Source: Isham, Narayan, and Pritchett 1995.

Civil liberties matter for economic projects.

Figure 4.2 Civil Liberties and the Probability of World Bank Project Failure

Probability of failure

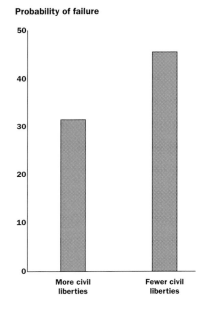

Source: Isham, Kaufmann, and Pritchett 1997.

Economica Federal, this project uses an effective sewage collection strategy. "PROSANEAR boasts a high degree of community participation and shared responsibility. Communities are increasingly involved in monitoring household use and system performance, and in managing their own repairs. The project's most striking feature is Caixa's commitment to adjust design and works according to the lessons of experience" (World Bank 1995a, p. 6).

Public Sector Compensation and Performance

The approach to aid that emphasized the quantity of investment and technocratic skills tended to underestimate the power of incentives in determining the actions of public sector providers. In the past donor and government technocrats assumed that once power plants were built, they would be operated effectively; new roads would be maintained; health clinics, once constructed, would provide quality services. In reality benefits will flow only if there are adequate incentives for (mainly civil service) providers. Both bilateral and multilateral donors now recognize that incentives are crucial for success and have been providing support for reforms in public sector management and the civil service.

Many poor countries have found it hard to maintain a competent, efficient, and honest civil service because real public sector wages have tumbled in the past 15–20 years. Underpaid (but not especially overworked) and with their morale at rock bottom, civil servants, especially high-level ones, have turned to moonlighting and corruption (World Bank 1995b). By 1986 the real average wage in Tanzania, for example, had fallen to a fifth of its 1969–77 value. The wage of top civil servants had fallen even further: to just 6 percent of its previous level. The ratio of top level pay to the minimum wage was only five to one. Pay is not always the problem. Even in countries where civil service pay is adequate, the structure of incentives is not. Guarantees of job tenure and lockstep pay rises based on seniority encourage none but the workaholic.

Especially in poor and aid-dependent economies, donors have sometimes done more harm than good. In their efforts to attract the best people for projects, donors can unwittingly deplete the civil service of its best and brightest, offering salaries and working conditions that governments cannot match. An independent study reported that for an agriculture project in Kenya the World Bank hired eight local people at salaries of $3,000–6,000 a month; of the eight, all but one was recruited from the civil service, where the monthly salary for a senior economist was roughly $250. In Mozambique international organizations were paying five times the civil service wage for professional staff and 10 times the civil service wage for technicians (Fallon and Pereira da Silva 1995). The combination of low civil service salaries and competition for skilled personnel among donors makes the strengthening of the civil service through training a Herculean task. Workers leave as quickly as they are trained. One program in Kenya funded by the Canadian International Development Agency trained 13 economists to the master's level; within a year, 10 had found jobs outside government, and the other three were searching (van de Walle and Johnston 1996).

Civil service reform, too, often denudes the public sector of its most competent staff. Reforms usually include downsizing (jargon for eliminating redundancies). When this is "voluntary"(employees are offered a severance package, usually more generous than mandated by law), the most skilled are the first to leave. But downsizing does not have to be a problem. In 1991 Peru announced two staff reduction packages for its civil service. One was an across-the-board offer taken up by 250,000 workers, of which 163,000 had to be rehired later. In contrast, the downsizing in tax administration targeted employees by skill level and was able to reduce staff by two-thirds while raising wages and doubling tax revenue (Haltiwanger and Singh forthcoming).

Effective Public Institutions

When donor-financed projects fail, it is often because of weak institutions and public organizations. There is plenty of evidence that institutional capability affects overall economic growth and the success of investments. One recent study found that over the 30 years to 1994, countries with sound policies and capable and effective government institutions grew at 3 percent per capita each year—while those with sound policies but weak institutions grew at only 1.4 percent a year (World Bank 1997a).

Using an index based on various dimensions of government performance, a recent staff review of World Bank–financed projects found that, whereas the average success rate on Bank projects was 68 percent, projects in countries with sound policies and capable institutions had an 86 percent success rate. Countries with neither sound policies nor able institutions had failures in 52 percent of projects, nearly four times the rate in countries with good policies and governance (see overview figure 5).

When donor-financed projects fail, it is often because of weak institutions and public organizations.

89

This study concludes that: "in settings where policies and institutions are seriously weak, the Bank would do best to focus on policy-based lending and non-lending services that support the strategic policy-making and implementation capacity of government"(World Bank 1997a, p. 13).

Would better-designed official development assistance mean more effective public institutions? Because aid has gone almost exclusively to (or through) central governments, it has affected how public services are delivered. In general, government-provided services are those that are difficult to allocate via markets, either because they are pure public goods that benefit all (national security, rule of law) or because they involve external effects that are hard to value (health services, environmental protection). The nature of these services, however, implies problems in designing lasting institutions and incentives for efficient public sector delivery and performance.

In the interests of effective implementation, donors often establish quasi-independent project implementation units outside the line ministry (and sometimes outside the government). Donors do this to "cocoon" the projects they finance from the worst inadequacies of the public sector. When projects are "successfully"concluded and turned over for operation to the regular line ministry, they lack the commitment, competence, and resources needed to continue. While isolating projects can at times make sense for purposes of piloting, demonstration, or evaluation, narrowly measured implementation "success" that comes at the expense of institutional capacity building generally is a Pyrrhic victory and inimical to the true success of aid.

The design of projects needs to adjust to the reality that money or capital stock is less important than good institutions or better ideas.

The design of projects needs to adjust to the reality that money or capital stock is less important than good institutions or better ideas. The point of an education project is not to increase funding for the sector (this can be done without projects) but to help reformers change the ideas, institutions, and policies in the sector. A truly effective project is a bundle of activities that does not just build schools but, more important, helps to change how schools are run to provide high-quality education. Building the finest schools, hospitals, or roads is pointless if the institutional capacity does not exist to maintain and run them.

This means that the most useful projects will often be innovative. If a country is competent at building schools and running them, donors should simply provide general budgetary support. The only rationale for a project is that things should be done differently than they are now. If existing schools are ineffective, a useful project might rehabilitate them and help alter institutional arrangements (for example, increasing community input into decisionmaking). Such a project may draw on things that have worked elsewhere, but it is innovative in the setting where it is being implemented.

An important corollary is that the success rate of financed projects is not particularly relevant—if success is narrowly defined. An effective agency may finance a lot of innovative projects, and some of these may "fail"—in the sense that they do not lead to better services. The important question is whether developing countries are systematically gaining knowledge from such experiments. Failed projects can often teach as much (or more than) successful ones. If projects are deemed "successful" because they merely replicate past success, agencies have the wrong incentives to provide effective assistance. Managers will want to avoid risky, innovative projects in favor of things that are known to work. This leads to unseemly and counterproductive competition among donors to "skim the cream" and finance only those items in the public investment program that are likely to be successful—with or without donor involvement.

In response, donor agencies have moved to broader measures of project success. They typically assess the effect of projects on the institutional capacity of sector agencies. Take a road project. Are better technologies for designing and building roads being introduced? Will pricing and other policies ensure maintenance? Are agency staff receiving necessary training? Assessing whether there is a "substantial institutional effect" is essentially asking a host of questions about whether the project is helping the recipient country to change the way that it manages its road sector.

Note that a project could have a successful "outcome"—the road is built and has a high return—but no lasting effect. On the flip side, a project could have "failed" but have led to substantial institutional development. This is particularly true of innovative approaches to service delivery, to which a lot of aid now goes. The innovative approach may not work, but if it is systematically evaluated and the knowledge is fed into a broader reform program, the project is helping improve the management of the sector.

This kind of serious impact evaluation has often been missing from development assistance, yet it is potentially of the greatest value. Again, innovations may fail, but development assistance is strengthening the underlying institutions by assisting in the design and evaluation of new approaches and generation of knowledge. Increasingly, donors are emphasizing the crucial importance of this kind of knowledge creation. Witness the United Kingdom. A recent White Paper on International Development says:

If projects are deemed "successful" because they merely replicate past success, agencies have the wrong incentives to provide effective assistance.

91

Without research, many development interventions would fail or be much less successful.

"Research is an important weapon in the fight against poverty. Without research, many development interventions would fail or be much less successful; and research has significant multiplier effects—solutions to the causes of poverty in one part of the developing world may well be replicable in another. The principle of shared knowledge is an important component of the partnerships which are essential to development. The Government sees the continued investment in knowledge generation as a key element in achieving its aims and objectives for international development" (U.K. White Paper 1997, p. 48).

At the World Bank, each completed project is rated on the basis of whether it had a "substantial institutional development impact," and this is viewed as the "most important evaluation criteria for long-term development effectiveness" (World Bank 1997a, p. 24). However, this component is also difficult. For a long time the share of World Bank–financed projects with a "substantial" institutional impact hovered around 30 percent, and only in recent years has it climbed to 39 percent. Thus it is possible for development projects to help change significantly the way the public sector does business. But it still happens in too few cases.

In our view, an effective development agency will be taking risks, systematically evaluating the outcomes, and disseminating the knowledge gained. This generation and dissemination of knowledge is one of the biggest contributions that development assistance can make. In tandem with the old rationale for aid, in which donor financing addressed market failure in capital markets, donor activities need to address the market failure in "knowledge" markets (Stiglitz 1988). But serious, rigorous evaluations that generate solid knowledge are expensive, and no one government has the incentive to undertake evaluations that will benefit other countries.

Public Provision without Public Providers

To make aid more effective, developing country governments are increasingly turning away from the traditional (and exclusive) use of public bureaucracies to provide services. Many public services can be provided effectively (often more effectively) by private organizations under contract or holding a concession. Donors and governments have often turned to nongovernmental organizations. New sources of financing have also brought about important changes in providers' incentives, empowered intended beneficiaries, and so increased the effectiveness of aid.

Contracting and Concessions

Privatizations and divestments have reduced the drain on government revenues and capacity in areas where public sector involvement is not critical. But even when government retains responsibility for services, they need not be managed through the usual public sector agency. Many activities can be contracted out to the private sector, and competition among potential providers can create pressures for cost-effectiveness.

How does it work? Take AGETIPs (Agences d'Execution des Travaux d'Interêt Public), not-for-profit associations that enter into contractual arrangements with governments to carry out infrastructure projects. The first was in Senegal, which (by contracting with individual suppliers through open bids) was able to reduce costs and delays. Other West African countries soon adopted this model (World Bank 1997c).

A concession is a way to contract with private providers for the provision of services without relinquishing public ownership of assets or public control of service delivery conditions. In Guinea a contractual arrangement under which a private management agency took over the operation of a water system was set up with the help of an International Development Association loan that initially paid the difference between costs and the revenues recovered from users. The subsidy was gradually reduced and the operation is now run commercially. This shows how aid can smooth the introduction of new arrangements. As important, donors can relay positive (and negative) experiences to other aid agencies and countries contemplating similar arrangements—be it power deregulation in Chile, water concessions in Argentina, or toll roads in Mexico.

Disseminating experience and lessons from innovators is especially important in improving the effectiveness of aid. Take railways, a clear example of diffusion of information about innovations in management. In developing countries railways are often run down and costly, with outdated rolling stock—all thanks to inefficient public management and competition from roads and airlines. Argentina was an innovator in railways. It split its massive federal system into several freight and commuter rail networks and awarded the rights to run them to private firms, some-

Many public services can be provided effectively (often more effectively) by private organizations under contract or holding a concession.

times through "negative"concessions (where firms bid the lowest amount the government would have to offer them in subsidies). While some of these concessions have had problems, labor productivity quadrupled, prices fell, and the public sector saved $600 million (Thompson and Budin 1997). More important for aid, development agencies helped ensure that the pitfalls and pluses of Argentina's experience were incorporated into programs in Brazil, Chile, Mexico, and countries in Africa, which have all moved to concession railways.

NGOs as Service Providers

The use of nongovernmental organizations (NGOs) as implementing agencies for donor-financed projects is another rising trend (box 4.2). Many NGOs also receive government contracts to provide services.

NGOs have advantages in providing some services, over both government agencies and more profit-oriented suppliers. NGOs can often reach local and target groups more effectively than can traditional government agencies. But NGOs are no cure for the shortcomings of the public sector. Moreover, external NGOs often have the same problem as donors in

---

Box 4.2   A Useful Surge in Nongovernmental Organizations

A RECENT REPORT BY JAPAN'S OVERSEAS ECONOMIC Cooperation Fund (OECF) notes that "the spread of democracy and the broader political participation that has come with the end of the Cold War has stimulated NGO activity throughout the world. The governments of both developing and industrial countries have a relatively good understanding of the large role that NGOs can play in a country's development. The OECF has collaborated with local NGOs on preimplementation studies and project implementation for several projects, including the Aravalli Hills Afforestation Project in India and the Forest Sector Project in the Philippines. It has also commissioned a Japanese

NGO, the Japan Wild Bird Society, to conduct an environmental survey on the habitat of cranes as part of the OECF's special assistance for project formation for the Development Project of Agriculture on State Farms in Heilongjiang Province in China (Sanjiang Plain). For the Jamuna Multipurpose Bridge Project in Bangladesh, a local NGO is conducting the basic survey on site expropriation. There have also been numerous instances in which local and international NGOs have contributed valuable advice on sector surveys, preimplementation studies, and project appraisal and implementation" (OECF 1996, p. 60).

creating sustainability and local ownership (World Bank 1998 a). So, while NGOs can be part of the service delivery system, they cannot replace government and cannot be a permanent substitute for public sector capacity.

User Fees, Effectiveness, and Demand-side Financing

Government services (particularly those financed by aid) are often provided free to users—health care, irrigation, water, extension services, schooling, roads, and so on. In many cases this approach is socially desirable but raises three problems—two serious, one less so. Least important, free services tend to be overused, clogging the system—be it a road network or health clinic. The two more severe problems are institutional and closely related to aid. First, since the service does not generate revenues, its provider depends on the general treasury for funding. Especially in poor countries with chronic or recurrent fiscal crises, that is cold comfort. There is little assurance that funds needed for, say, medicine or irrigation maintenance will be forthcoming. Second, because funding comes from the treasury, it is difficult to empower beneficiaries or instill in them the sense of ownership so necessary for the success of aid projects. Users are frozen out, in setting priorities and planning and delivering services.

In recent years donors have financed innovative ways to increase service effectiveness by creating charges directly linked to improvements in quality —from irrigation to education, health to agriculture. Health is a good example. Providing universal health care in poor countries is a laudable aim. But because of insufficient funding, morale is in the depths, and more important, clinics often have no needles, drugs, or medicine. That leads to a vicious cycle: patients, knowing the poor quality, seek care elsewhere, leading to underuse of clinics, which makes it harder to justify increased budgets to improve services (Filmer, Hammer, and Pritchett 1998).

In 1988 the Bamako Initiative sought to reverse that cycle by introducing user fees in Cameroon. A project financed by the U.S. Agency for International Development carried out a controlled evaluation of the combination of charging user fees and using them to improve quality by creating a reliable drug supply. The study found that not only did the use of health centers increase but that there were proportionately more poor users than rich (Litvack and Bodart 1993). Similar experiments have had similar results in other sectors, such as education (Birdsall and Orivel 1996). Examples like these reveal the valuable role donors can play in financing and evaluating innovations in service delivery.

In recent years donors have financed innovative ways to increase service effectiveness.

Making Aid Work for Better Public Services

The shift in development thinking requires reorienting the instruments of aid.

THE SHIFT IN DEVELOPMENT THINKING FROM A GOVERNMENT-LED accumulationist strategy to a focus on fundamentals, effectiveness, and efficiency in core public sector responsibilities requires reorienting the instruments of aid. In particular, it means reconsidering the methods of financial (project and program) and nonfinancial (technical assistance, policy analysis, training) assistance and how they can be adapted to support the new development strategy.

Project Finance

We have not yet discussed a topic that accounts for most of the analysis of aid effectiveness: the technical and administrative details of making aid projects more effective. There are two reasons for this. First, and most important, this area has been well covered in many past evaluations, reviews of experience, and research, and we have little of value to add. Many donor agencies review the performance of completed projects. The combination of individual project experience and comparisons across countries allows these evaluations to provide critical and constructive suggestions from the lessons learned to improve the organization's operations. In addition, some donor agencies' technical departments and evaluation departments produce sector specific reviews of both the problems faced and promising approaches in each sector.[1] This voluminous literature on project performance and sectors provides a wealth of information needed to implement successful projects.

The second reason that we do not go further into the issue of effective aid projects is that we are more interested in the indirect than the direct effects of projects. Aid-financed projects can have spillover effects from individual projects to the general operation of the public sector.

Almost from the beginning, projects financed by foreign aid were thought to have important indirect and broader benefits. Hirschmann (1967) argued that perhaps the greatest were institutional and personal learning from the conception, planning, and implementation of projects. He believed that projects were the "privileged particles" of development that created innovation by confronting problems as they arise. These benefits emphasize the value added of donor involvement, which allows a supportive "infrastructure" of institutional and technical support for implementation that would otherwise not be present.

Development projects can be a testing ground for ideas or concepts that are new to a country, demonstrating to the government and citizens what does (or does not) work—contracting out public services, using NGOs, involving user groups in management, and so on. The value added of donors is twofold. One is the ability to devote resources to careful evaluation of experience. Knowledge of this type is an international public good, and no government has sufficient incentive to evaluate or disseminate it. Donor projects can also help break the mentality that locks the public sector into ineffective arrangements. Reform-minded governments find it hard to implement new ideas—especially those that challenge entrenched interests, particularly if there is no guarantee that they will work. That they will work can often only be proven by implementation. Donors can break this vicious circle by helping to implement such projects. In a joint meeting of officials of the Gambia and the World Bank to improve the working relationship, the Gambians expressed "the importance of the Bank's role in bringing experience and ideas from outside as the strongest plank in the partnership. Financing was vital, but more because it represented the possibility to do—moving beyond talk" (Marshall 1997, p. 26).

But the benefits depend on the project being implemented in a way that is different and on the evaluation of this difference. Unfortunately, both of these requirements are rarely met, as donor-financed projects often do not provide mechanisms for rigorous evaluation of outcomes—or did not until recently.

Projects also present opportunities to engage in a sectorwide dialogue with government. Many investment project failures are linked to sector policies of government that often conflict and work at cross-purposes. For instance, in some countries agricultural extension, irrigation, and transport projects intended to encourage farmers to grow specific crops have been overwhelmed by macroeconomic and microeconomic policies that effectively resulted in heavy taxation on agriculture. In other countries investments in roads, irrigation, and other infrastructure have been poorly maintained (or not maintained at all) because public agencies could not recover costs and were starved of funds. Changes in general policies that result from dialogue improve the sustainability of donor-financed projects and improve prospects for all projects in the sector. This effect can be crucial value added from donor involvement.

Just one example comes from the difficult area of resettlement caused by land acquisitions in public investments (see box 4.3). Because projects can have both a direct impact (a new road links communities, carries

Development projects can be a testing ground for ideas or concepts that are new to a country.

97

people and freight) and spillover benefits (improving institutions and sector policies), both need to be evaluated.

Nonproject Finance

Donor financing that is tied less to the implementation of particular projects—such as program aid, sector investment financing, sectoral adjustment programs, or other time-slice finance instruments—has advantages and disadvantages over project finance.

In a country where spending allocations are sound and the effectiveness of expenditures is high, the potential value added of donor involvement in project design and implementation is minimal. Nonproject financing saves on project preparation and implementation costs, both for donors and recipient governments. One scarce resource of donors is staff with technical skills and experience from a range of countries. Since project preparation is staff intensive, however, using projects as a form of support in well-managed countries does not necessarily allocate staff where their skills are best used or needed. Scarce skills will probably be put to more productive use elsewhere. For recipients, nonproject assis-

---

Box 4.3   Resettlement in Development

A COMPREHENSIVE REVIEW OF THE WORLD Bank's experience with implementing its resettlement policies in its projects concludes that:

"Having been the first international development agency ever to adopt a resettlement policy, the Bank has promoted this policy with the Borrowers whose projects include involuntary population displacement. One main result of the Bank's catalytic impact 1986 to 1993 is that several Borrowers enacted or improved domestic policies and legal frameworks for resettlement.

"Resettlement works when governments want it to work. The main way governments express their commitments to good resettlement is by creating adequate institutional capacity, defined as the synergy between policies, organizations, and resources.

When borrowers do not genuinely concur with the Bank's resettlement policy from the outset, resettlement is generally not carried out well—regardless of Bank missions or the frequency of Bank threats to suspend disbursements.

"The Bank has been far more effective overall—and immediate operations have benefited more—when it in reached agreement with borrowing governments on the broad domestic or sector policy framework relevant to Bank-assisted operations, than when its efforts were confined to legal agreements for individual projects. In turn, the obligations it laid down in individual loan legal agreements and the agreed "project policy" have sometimes formed the basis for discussing and improving more general domestic legal and policy frameworks" (World Bank 1996a, p. 8).

tance helps with donor coordination. The administrative setup needed to monitor perhaps hundreds of donor-financed projects is burdensome to governments with limited public sector management capability. Often each donor and each project has its own procedures, plans, and reporting and procurement requirements.

Project financing brings its own biases into the incentives of aid agencies: favoring investment over recurrent spending, large projects over small ones, expansion of physical production over improvement in efficiency, imported materials over domestic. Recipients often see projects as being generated and implemented by aid agencies alone, with little local ownership.

The use of general budgetary support delinks projects and implementation from overall targets for assistance—that is, the size of projects is often scaled to meet targets for total assistance disbursed rather than to maximize the value added of projects. At times the scale of the project works at cross-purposes with its intent.

But all of these considerations apply mainly to those lucky few countries and sectors in which public services are already effective and, perhaps, even efficient. If one of the main concerns of development is to improve policies and increase government's institutional capacity (and it should be), foreign assistance that simply expands the budget envelope of existing activities without changing the structure or incentives for service delivery is unlikely to see much of a payoff. The question is: What kind of support will best lead to public sector improvement? Sometimes projects are necessary. At other times a policy dialogue—connected to program assistance—is needed. And sometimes no financing at all is the most useful.

An excellent study of aid in Africa sponsored by the Overseas Development Council, based on collaborative case studies in seven African countries, makes this recommendation:

Project financing brings its own biases into the incentives of aid agencies: favoring investment over recurrent spending, large projects over small.

"[Program aid] is not likely to promote development in the absence of sound economic policies. In such situations, donors should maintain a policy dialogue with the government, but limit aid flows and direct them to project assistance, often focusing on non-state actors. When sound economic policies have been put in place, donors should expand program aid, perhaps in the context of sectoral investment strategies negotiated with the government"(van de Walle and Johnston 1996, p. 8).

A society (or government agency) that has generated its own reform program is receptive to technical assistance and institution building.

This recognizes the complex factors in the choice of the method and level of development assistance. Effective aid depends not just on the type and method of aid chosen, but critically on government policies, institutional capability, and commitment to improve services.

Nonfinancial Support

Nonfinancial support can have a high payoff, but its record has been mixed. Lack of institutional capacity in developing countries has long been recognized as a big hurdle to development.[2] One traditional solution has been to use three types of technical assistance: employing foreign experts on a short- or long-term basis, training government officials (in country or abroad), and financing long-run educational programs. While donors have made much use of foreign experts to improve institutions (and there have been successes) the overall results have been disappointing (World Bank 1996b). A United Nations Development Programme evaluation in 1993 suggested that "there is a growing sense that technical cooperation does not work well, that as presently practiced it is ineffective, that such benefits as it brings are extremely costly, and that in any case it has little lasting impact" (Berg 1993, p. 3–4).

A society (or government agency) that has generated its own reform program is receptive to technical assistance and institution building. When not driven by domestic demand for particular expertise, however, foreign experts are often not integrated with ministries in a way that allows knowledge to be transferred. Free-standing technical assistance provided by international consultants and individual technical experts has served some purposes, but as a way to promote and improve public sector institutions they have usually been expensive failures.

Training government officials in technical tasks has also had mixed results. In many countries training has been unsuccessful because public officials do not have the incentive to perform, are politically blocked from performing, or do not have the materials or resources to perform. In many countries there is no way to speed up the slow process that involves creating not just the capacity for policy analysis and dialogue (both in government and civil society) but also the demand from recipient governments for productive technical assistance. The impact of ideas is difficult to monitor, evaluate, and especially quantify because the ways in which policy analysis contributes to future performance are often intangible and indirect.

One study undertook an empirical analysis of World Bank projects (mostly approved in the 1980s) to investigate the relative contribution of two staff inputs (Deininger, Squire, and Basu 1998). One is the input directly related to the project—preparation before the project begins and supervision while the project is being implemented and the finance is being disbursed. The second is "economic and sector work," which produces reports on the economy and particular sectors for government but also covers the dialogue with government and other development agencies.

The study found that (even after controlling for country, sector, and economic conditions and staff preparation and supervision for a particular project) prior analytical work improves projects. On average these activities have a high payoff, as the benefit of one additional week of analytical work by the World Bank is nine times the cost—including staff time, travel, and overhead (figure 4.3). Moreover, since analytical work affects many projects, the overall benefit is even larger. And these are just the payoffs to projects financed by the Bank. If the changes made from policy analysis affect other donor-financed projects, or perhaps even all government projects, the returns to involvement in nonlending activities would be enormous.

While analytical work has a high return, the same authors found that the World Bank underinvested in it, and overinvested in resources dedicated to ensure that a steady stream of projects went to the Executive Board (appendix 5). According to their estimates, a shift of resources from project preparation to analytical work would have led to lower commitments but a higher success rate of projects. In other words, fewer projects would have been approved, but they would have been better designed and better implemented. Ironically, a shift of resources from project preparation to analytical work would have led to higher—not lower—disbursements of funds. The reason is that problem projects are implemented slowly and hence disburse slowly.

The payoffs for analytical work can be enormous.

Figure 4.3 Cost and Benefit of an Additional Week of Analytical Work

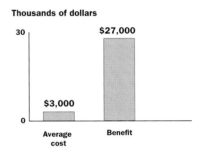

Source: Deininger, Squire, and Basu 1998.

Methods of Assistance and Public Sector Efficiency

Properly managed, aid can encourage better public sectors through both project and nonproject activities (and often through a combination of the two). Both can provide the knowledge countries need. Projects support experimentation and reform, demonstration, piloting, evaluation, and innovation. There are also several ways in which donors can assist countries through nonproject activities, such as by creating and diffusing

Properly managed, aid can encourage better public sectors through both project and nonproject activities.

information drawn from their experience. Since aid agencies implement many projects in different countries and with different institutional structures and have an established capacity to evaluate projects, they can draw on cross-cutting evidence and experience that no single country could. Policy analysis, bringing technical expertise to bear, can be useful. Training—that is, enabling domestic actors with the necessary capabilities to accomplish their objectives, whether by exposing policymakers to other experiences or providing new skill—also plays a key role.

Notes

1. Even a partial list of the literature produced by just the World Bank gives some indication. From the Operations Evaluation Department have come reviews of, among other sectors, irrigation, agricultural extension, and adjustment lending. Sectoral policy papers reviewing the experience with Bank involvement have been produced on, among others, energy, water, education, and adjustment lending.

2. Krueger, Michalopoulos, and Ruttan (1989) note that in the 1950s the U.S. Agency for International Development was home to a huge debate between advocates of capital assistance and advocates of technical assistance.

CHAPTER 5

Money, but More Ideas, Too

G OOD ECONOMIC MANAGEMENT MATTERS MORE TO developing countries than foreign financial aid does. Policy and institutional gaps hold back economies that lag behind, not financing gaps. Aid money has a big impact only after countries have made substantial progress in reforming their policies and institutions. These messages should not, however, be twisted to mean that countries with weak institutions and policies (call them difficult, weak, or troubled environments) cannot be helped. They can. Many things can be done usefully.

The international community needs to get beyond projects and spur systemic change in whole sectors and countries.

But first we know from experience what is *unlikely* to work:

- *Large amounts of money.* Providing significant financing has not made much of a dent in poverty in countries with weak management.
- *Buying reform.* Conditional lending has not generated reform in countries with no domestic movement in this direction for reform.
- *Focusing on individual projects.* In difficult environments donors have often fallen back on a core program of projects, mostly in the social sectors. But the success of individual projects (always difficult to achieve) does not have much impact unless it spurs *systemic change.* And because money typically is fungible, the whole (distorted) public sector is being financed, not just the favored sector.

So, the international community needs to get beyond projects and spur systemic change in whole sectors and countries. Easier said than done. Almost nothing positive has happened in Myanmar (Burma) or Nigeria in the past three decades. There obviously is no panacea for the ills of such countries. Even so, there are examples of successful assistance that has improved the lives of people living in countries with weak governance and poor policies. In some cases this assistance has contributed to a larger transformation that made a major difference.

Here we present four case studies of effective aid under difficult conditions. Running through them are four themes:

In difficult environments, effective assistance is more about ideas than money or projects.

- *Find a champion.* Countries, governments, and communities are heterogeneous. While it is fair to characterize Burma overall as "poorly managed," there are likely to be reform-minded elements in the community and even in the government. If aid can find and support these reformers, it can have a big impact.
- *Have a long-term vision of systemic change.* Successful reformers have a vision of how things could be different in, say, 10 years—different both in outcomes (more kids going to school, graduating, getting jobs) and in process (community involvement in schools, broad public support for reform policies).
- *Support knowledge creation.* While reformers typically have a long-term vision, they often need to develop the details of reform through innovation and evaluation. Moreover, for reform to take root requires a demonstration that it works. Financing and evaluating innovations is a key role for development assistance.
- *Engage civil society.* In highly distorted environments the government is failing to provide supportive policies and effective services. That is why government-to-government financial transfers produce poor results. Effective aid in such an environment often involves supporting civil society to pressure the government to change or to take service provision directly into its own hands (or to do both).

The foregoing points deal with the characteristics of promising environments for change and the ways donors can enhance those characteristics. The lessons from successful assistance also provide guidance about donor behavior. Aid is more effective when:

- *Agencies focus on long-term reform.* Successful aid in difficult environments typically involves intensive staff input from donors and small disbursements of money. It also goes "beyond projects" to support systemic reforms. In difficult environments, effective assistance is more about ideas than money or projects.

■ *Donors work as partners rather than competitors.* Studies of aid have long pointed to the proliferation of donors and the lack of coordination among them. Well-managed countries force coordination on donors, but in the weak environments donors often run amok. It is hard to explain this, except that different donors like to "plant their flags" on something (anything) tangible. In cases of successful assistance, there tends to be a strong partnership among donors with a focus on larger transformations, not on individual flags.

Well-managed countries force coordination on donors, but in the weak environments donors often run amok.

Vietnam: Adjustment without Lending

IT WOULD BE HARD TO IMAGINE A TOUGHER ENVIRONMENT FOR development assistance than Vietnam in the mid-1980s. One of the world's poorest countries, Vietnam had to appeal for international food aid at several points in the decade. Despite Soviet aid (10 percent of GNP each year), there was virtually no progress in development (in poverty reduction or improved social indicators). Economic management was poor. The trade regime was closed. There was no scope in the economy for the private sector. And a large fiscal imbalance was financed by printing money, leading to hyperinflation.

Vietnam in 1985–86 is a good example of how a large amount of financial aid can have no impact in an environment of distorted institutions and policies. There was widespread dissatisfaction within society, government, and the ruling communist party with these poor results. At a landmark meeting in 1986 the party decided to change direction and initiated *doi moi* (renovation). One of the leading champions of reform was Vo Van Kiet, who emerged as deputy prime minister responsible for the economy. The impetus for change came not just from the fact that Vietnam was doing poorly, but from the success of nearby economies that were more open to foreign trade and investment. Although the economic team had a general sense of the direction for economic policy—toward more private initiative and greater openness—it did not have a detailed reform program (Ljunggren 1993).

The Soviet Union's aid dropped sharply in the late 1980s, leaving Vietnam with only limited assistance (less than 1 percent of GDP) primarily from the UNDP and Sweden (SIDA). While Vietnam was grappling with classic adjustment problems, it was receiving no financial

Vietnam's reform opened more space for civil society, and donor activities encouraged this as well.

support from the IMF or the World Bank because of its political estrangement from the major shareholders of these institutions. The two were, however, contributing some staff time to advise the government. Furthermore, UNDP and SIDA invited the Bank and the Fund to manage some of the technical assistance they financed. So, the IMF managed UNDP-financed technical assistance for the central bank and contributed some of its own staff time. In a similar arrangement the World Bank managed UNDP-financed assistance for the State Planning Committee (now the Ministry of Planning and Investment).

In the early stages of reform this partnership of agencies provided important inputs. In 1991 the UNDP and the World Bank organized a meeting in Kuala Lumpur at which Vo Van Kiet and his team met with economic ministers from Indonesia, the Republic of Korea, and Malaysia. Each country laid out some key policies that had worked for them, and the Vietnamese team asked detailed questions about stabilization, trade liberalization, foreign investment, and other economic policies. At a more technical level, the same group of donor agencies organized training courses, policy workshops, and study tours for staff from Vietnam's economic ministries.

All this was aimed at helping Vietnam learn about its neighbors' experiences and develop the knowledge it needed to manage its own economy successfully. The generation of knowledge was supported at a more micro level, too. UNDP, SIDA, and the World Bank teamed to help the government carry out the first representative household survey ever done in Vietnam—generating a wealth of information about household production, income and poverty, education, health, and child nutrition. This survey, conducted in 1992–93, revealed that 55 percent of the population lived below a widely used international poverty line (Dollar and others 1998).

Vietnam's reform opened more space for civil society, and donor activities encouraged this as well. Two examples: The Asia Foundation and the World Bank organized the first public meeting between the domestic private sector and leading officials to discuss economic policies and key distortions holding back private investment. And a group of donors organized rural workshops to discuss the poverty analysis that emerged from the household survey and how donors could support local initiatives aimed at poverty reduction.

It is impossible to measure the exact effect of these donor activities. But there undoubtedly has been dramatic improvement in economic policies in Vietnam and that has made people's lives better. Vietnam's

Figure 5.1 Vietnam: Aid and Policy

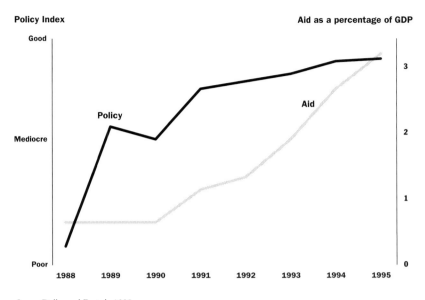

Source: Dollar and Easterly 1998.

Aid in Vietnam focused on policy advice and technical assistance during adjustment and reform. Large-scale finance arrived after a good policy framework was in place.

policy improved from truly terrible in the mid-1980s to merely poor by 1990 (figure 5.1). (The improvement captures the strengthening of property rights over agricultural land and the first stage of stabilization, going from 400 percent inflation to about 70 percent.) There was further steady policy improvement in the early 1990s as inflation was brought under control, trade liberalized, and the legal environment for the private sector clarified.

Note that during 1989–93 Vietnam was receiving a small amount of aid (about 1 percent of GDP). Large-scale financial aid did not arrive until 1994–95, by which time the institutional and policy environment was quite good for a low-income country.

Vietnam is a good example of systemic change. In the mid-1980s households were restricted in what they could do with land and labor. By the mid-1990s they had considerable freedom to work their land, start a household business, or look for wage labor. Innovations that had worked well locally were "scaled up" to the whole country. With the better policy environment came the need for complementary investments in roads, power, education, and other sectors.

In the wake of policy reform, growth accelerated. Of the 40 poorest countries in the world in 1986, Vietnam had by far the fastest growth

In recent years many developing countries have experimented with decentralization of education.

in the next decade. And benefits have been widely shared. A 1998 study of the households first surveyed in 1992–93 revealed that average household income had risen 39 percent in real terms and that the poverty rate had been cut nearly in half—from 55 percent of households to about 30 percent.

What are the lessons for foreign aid? Donors helped a reformer develop policies for Vietnam and show that they could work. And the clear objectives of Vietnam's leaders helped in coordinating donors.

The focus during the critical 1989–92 period was clearly on ideas, not money. For reasons of international politics, major donors such as the World Bank could not provide money to Vietnam until 1993, so they had to do something different. Intensive staff time required little money and made a big contribution to the country's reform and development.

El Salvador, Pakistan, and Brazil: Education's Decentralization and Reform

GOVERNMENTS IN DEVELOPING COUNTRIES USUALLY PLAY A MAJOR role in the allocation and management of educational resources. Even when some authority is delegated to provinces or municipalities, individual school administrators and parents have a limited voice. This centralized approach has supported many achievements in education, but it has not always reached groups that have traditionally had low levels of education (the poor and girls, for instance). And overcentralization can stifle initiative among those critical in affecting school outcomes—teachers, principals, and parents.

In recent years many developing countries have experimented with decentralization of education in two ways: first, allowing more local autonomy and input into public schools, and second, creating more space for the nongovernmental sector. In some cases donors have helped finance and design these innovations. Most important, there has been support for government efforts to evaluate these innovations seriously, following pilot groups and comparing them with control groups not participating in the pilot. For reforms in El Salvador, Pakistan, and Brazil, there is now solid evidence that they work.

El Salvador's community-managed schools program—more popularly known by the acronym, EDUCO, or *Educacion con Participation de la*

Comunidad—is an innovative effort for both preprimary and primary education to decentralize education by strengthening the direct involvement and participation of parents and community groups. A prototype of today's EDUCO schools emerged in the 1980s when public schools could not be extended to rural areas because of the country's civil war. Some communities took the initiative to organize their own schools, administered and financially supported by an association of households. Although these early attempts were held back by the low rural income base, they demonstrated a strong inherent demand for education as well as a desire to participate in the governance of schools. In 1991 El Salvador's ministry of education, supported by such aid agencies as the World Bank, decided to use the prototype as the principal method of expanding education in rural areas through the EDUCO program.

Today's EDUCO schools are managed autonomously by an elected community education association (*Association Comunal para la Education,* or ACE) drawn from the parents of the students. The ACEs take the central role of administration and management, and they are contracted by the ministry to deliver a given curriculum to an agreed number of students. The ACEs are then responsible for contracting and removing teachers' by closely monitoring their performance, and for equipping and maintaining the schools. The partnership between the ministry and the ACEs is expected to improve school administration and management by reflecting local needs.

The EDUCO program is a way to expand educational access quickly to remote rural areas. But has this come at the expense of quality? No. Community-managed schools are not low in quality. Student achievement on standardized mathematics and language tests is the same for EDUCO schools and traditional ones (after controlling for household background). In fact, EDUCO schools may be superior. They have significantly fewer school days missed by students as a result of teacher absence (Jimenez and Sawada 1998). Based on this success, the government is now planning to introduce community management into all traditional schools.

In Pakistan a long-standing problem has been the low participation of girls in schooling. In 1994–95 the provincial government of Balochistan began supporting nongovernmental schools, with an emphasis on increasing the enrollment of girls. Subsidies are paid to new nongovernmental schools, based on the number of girls enrolled. After three years, the schools are expected to be financially self-sufficient through fees and private support.

El Salvador's community-managed schools emerged in the 1980s when public schools could not be extended to rural areas because of the country's civil war.

An innovative program to support the start-up of girls' schools in Balochistan led to an immediate leap in girls' enrollment.

Figure 5.2 Pakistan: School Enrollment of Five- to Eight-year-old Girls

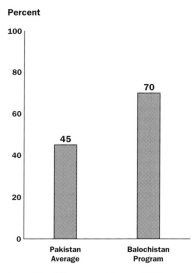

Source: Kim, Alderman, and Orazem 1998.

In urban areas a new private school was opened in every poor neighborhood randomly selected for the program. Girls' enrollment increased by 25 percentage points, compared with their enrollment in control group neighborhoods that did not participate in the program (figure 5.2). Moreover, even though the program provided a direct subsidy only to the enrollment of girls, it had a positive spillover effect on boys' enrollment. This success was not affected by income or other socio-economic characteristics of the neighborhood, suggesting that expanding it to other poor areas of Pakistan would likely be successful.

In rural areas, girls' enrollment is particularly low. So, the program supported the creation of girls' schools, often headed by a female teacher, a factor believed to significantly increase parents interest in sending their daughters to school. Again, results show that the program significantly increased girls' enrollment compared with villages without girls' schools. As in the urban areas, there has been a spillover benefit in higher boys' enrollment rates.

In Brazil's State of São Paulo the new secretary of education, Rose Neubauer, initiated decentralization and improvements in efficiency. The traditional system involved using the same building for primary school in the morning and secondary school in the afternoon, with teachers commuting among different schools. There were also the usual problems of low teacher salaries and morale. The result: low enrollment rates, many repeaters and dropouts, and poor student achievement.

The reforms were threefold. First, the system was rationalized. Remapping allowed the concentration of primary students in primary schools and secondary students in secondary schools. Teachers were thus assigned to a single school, reducing commuting time and creating a more coherent faculty. This freed up resources to lengthen the school day and increase teacher salaries. The state education budget increased by 10 percent, but teacher salaries nearly doubled—possible because of the efficiency gains.

Second was decentralization. The state handed responsibility for primary education to municipalities that had the resources, capacity, and desire to assume it. There was a further decentralization of authority to school heads. Previously, these were political appointees not always possessing the requisite skills. In the new system these heads have to take a pedagogical exam and develop an action plan for the school.

The third prong of the reform was a commitment to assessment and research—that is, to a "results focus." Serious evaluation enabled the government to determine quickly that the reforms were working. Within a few years primary school enrollments in municipalities doubled from 600,000 to 1.2 million. Repetition rates dropped from more than 10 percent to less than 4 percent. Dropout rates plunged from 9 percent to 5 percent in primary schools and from 20 percent to 12 percent in secondary schools. The ultimate test of reform will be its effect on student achievement, and the testing system will allow careful evaluation over the next few years. Early results are quite promising, and teachers are happier as well. Neubauer is the first secretary of education in more than 20 years to go three years without a teachers strike!

What can be learned from the El Salvador, Pakistan, and Brazil education reforms? In each case decentralizing and involving civil society led to improvements in public services—specifically, the broader availability of schooling to disadvantaged groups. A key issue in each case was to take a good idea and see if it worked, to create the potential for systemic change—that is, for the reform of the whole sector. In El Salvador and Brazil the government is moving in this direction. In Pakistan it remains to be seen if the innovation will be widely disseminated.

But for donors, these provide clear examples of how assistance can help support reformers—in the initial piloting, in serious impact evaluation, and in mainstreaming if there is demand to "scale up." Moreover, it is possible that these efforts to stimulate decentralization and community participation in education will have larger spillover benefits leading to more community involvement in other areas (roads, health), an important area for future study.

In El Salvador, Pakistan, and Brazil decentralizing and involving civil society led to improvements in public services.

Cameroon: Health Financing and Delivery

CAMEROON ENTERED THE 1980s WITH AN ANNUAL GROWTH RATE of 10 percent and exited them with an annual −10 percent growth. Partly the result of external shocks, the volatility was exacerbated by poor economic policy. The government adjusted slowly to a changed international environment and allowed its fiscal deficit to climb to an unsustainable 12 percent of GDP in 1988. The fiscal imbalance led the government to adopt structural adjustment measures, including a 19 percent reduction in total spending. As in other African countries faced with similar problems, expenditure cuts fell disproportionately on public investment and on nonsalary recurrent costs. The health budget declined by an even larger amount—46 percent in real terms between 1987 and 1990.

These cuts were one factor leading to low-quality health care and poor use of public health centers. The centers were left with a staff of four or five nurses but virtually no drugs or supplies. Not surprisingly, health personnel were demoralized. Only a few patients visited the health centers each day for curative care; and opportunities to deliver preventive health care decreased. Most people bypassed the health center and "self-treated" through traditional medicine or through purchasing drugs of dubious quality from private vendors, or through traveling to a distant town to buy expensive brand name drugs at a pharmacy.

Then, in 1989 the ministry of health decided to decentralize the administration and finance of rural health care delivery. The approach was similar to that being tried, with UNICEF support, in several other African countries. The ministry asked USAID to help design and make operational this reoriented approach to public health care in two provinces. Other donors and nongovernmental organizations (Germany's GTZ, UNICEF, CARE, Save the Children) were focusing on different aspects of primary health care. But the USAID-funded project was the pilot in which the government was experimenting with a comprehensive new approach to financing and delivering health services.

Local health committees were formed to oversee the operation of health centers and tell villagers about the importance of preventive health measures. Health centers were supplied with curative drugs and supplies, which were replenished through consultation fees and drug sales. Preventive health measures (vaccinations, family planning, information on safe drinking water) were still provided free.

By making good-quality, generic drugs available at health centers at a reasonable price it was thought that use of the centers would rise. In fact, the use of health centers increased significantly for households in areas with the new policy, but declined in the control group areas (figure 5.3). It was also thought that access of the poor might decline because of the user fees. But this did not happen. The poor were not left out. Indeed, they seemed to be benefiting proportionally more than others. Why? Because they lacked any source of reliable quality drugs prior to this policy, so it had a greater impact on them (Litvack and Bodart 1993).

Although this very successful pilot came to a close in 1994, opportunities for scaling up have not yet been realized. Many of the innovative

In a period of fiscal adjustment and expenditure cuts in Cameroon, health center use declined 16 percent. But in villages with an innovative program of user fees and revolving drug funds, use increased 9 percent.

Figure 5.3 Cameroon: Change in Health Center Use and Utilization, 1990–91

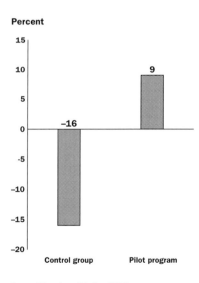

Source: Litvack and Bodart 1993.

policies implemented in the two provinces required a waiver of normal procedures, and to replicate the pilot throughout the country would require broader changes in policy and legislation. For example, it had been envisioned that every health committee would become a private, not-for-profit association with ministry representation to ensure its independence. The needed legislation was drafted during the course of the USAID-funded project, but it has yet to be presented to the National Assembly. Other issues need to be resolved before scaling up. How to address poorer areas; how to design transparent, predictable intergovernmental transfers to create incentives for cost recovery; and how to improve the central procurement system for pharmaceuticals.

What is the result of this partnership between reformers in the health sector and donor agencies? At least two provinces in Cameroon are delivering better health care to their people. Furthermore, there is a stock of knowledge that community participation with proper government support can be a powerful way to improve rural service delivery, particularly for the poor. This could be an important input into a larger reform program in the sector and beyond. But as yet there has been no broader reform, and it is difficult for donors to do much until there is a larger domestic movement for change.

Africa's road sector provides good examples of how money—in a weak institutional and policy environment—can have little impact.

Africa's Road Maintenance Initiative

AFRICA'S ROAD SECTOR PROVIDES GOOD EXAMPLES OF HOW MONEY —in a weak institutional and policy environment—can have little impact. Almost a third of Africa's $150 billion in roads (much of it aid-financed) has been lost due to lack of maintenance. Entering the 1990s about half the region's paved roads and 70 percent of the unpaved roads were in fair to poor condition. The poor state of the transport network was a serious bottleneck that lessened the value of reforms or other public investments.

Institutional and policy weaknesses prevented governments from providing necessary road maintenance despite ample funding. In most countries there was an almost exclusive reliance on public road maintenance companies, which tended to have a large capital stock (equipment) at low levels of use. The public sector companies were also overstaffed. Thus funds were directed at equipment and employment, but often were not available for other critical inputs (parts, fuel). The underlying problem: operations were used to meet objectives (say, employment) other than maintaining roads. Moreover, general weaknesses in national budgeting often led to an uneven flow of operating funds, further hampering efficiency.

In response to the mounting crisis, African transport ministers launched the Sub-Saharan Africa Transport Program in 1987, with the road maintenance initiative as a key component. The premise of the initiative is that the core problem of road maintenance is not technical or financial, but that the "real causes are weak and unsuitable institutional arrangements for managing and financing roads" (Heggie 1994, p. 2). The objective was to foster long-term systemic change, so that by 2000 countries would be well on their way to developing workable systems of maintenance.

The core problem of road maintenance is not technical or financial—it is weak and unsuitable institutional arrangements.

What were the initiative's innovative features? First, it began by bringing policymakers in the transport sector and road users together for seminars. Their focus was on the consequences of neglecting maintenance and on the institutional and policy weaknesses that resulted in poor maintenance. Countries discovered that they had common problems, and that already there were important examples of successful reform.

Second, the initiative focused on institutional weaknesses. The fact that road maintenance units were often part of the general civil service with inflexible employment policies, made it difficult to recruit, motivate, retain, or dismiss staff. Establishing autonomy for road agencies can provide more flexibility in employment. Financial autonomy can be important as well. In general, road maintenance is a public good, and road maintenance companies cannot directly charge the beneficiaries of their work. But taxes for vehicles and fuel can be structured to closely approximate "prices" for road construction and maintenance.

In a country with strong budget management a government may not want to earmark funds from vehicle and fuel taxes for road maintenance. (Whatever the source of the revenue, it should ideally go to the use that has the highest social return.) But the best can be the enemy of the good. If the budget is not well managed and funds do not flow to road maintenance—even when the return to the activity is extremely high—then it is wise to search for the institutional arrangement that best fits this case and provides a good outcome.

Some countries in the road maintenance initiative have started "road funds" in which certain taxes and fees are earmarked for road maintenance. This arrangement has benefits:

- It can improve tax collection. Collection always relies to a certain extent on the willingness of people to pay. When road users are convinced that their taxes are not going to provide public services, avoidance is high. If users are convinced that taxes will finance services that benefit them, they are more willing to pay.
- It can provide a steady financing source for day-to-day operations. In the past expensive equipment and staff could sit idle while the government resolved the latest fiscal crisis. In the new institutional arrangement, there is a more stable flow of funds.
- It can improve spending. Road funds are overseen by road boards that include both government staff from the sector as well as road users—farmers, businessmen, bus and transport companies. This partnership between the government and the private sector has led not just to better collection of road taxes but to more efficient use of funds.

The partnership between the government and the private sector has led not just to better collection of road taxes but to more efficient use of funds.

Road boards have also provided input into other institutional changes, moving away from exclusive reliance on the public sector to carry out road maintenance. There now are commercially run equipment pools, and both road maintenance tasks and equipment maintenance are being contracted out (Carapetis and others 1991).

One key lesson is the importance of having a long-term game plan for reform. The initiative began in 1987, but it came to show major results only in 1992. It also demonstrates the importance of "knowledge creation," as we use the term in this report. In highly distorted environments people stop expecting services from the public sector and become skeptical about possibilities for reform. What is needed in this situation is not just good ideas, but demonstrations that they work. Now that there is tangible evidence of their value, good ideas from the African road maintenance initiative are spreading quickly from country to country. Also needed for the reform of public institutions is the participation of civil society.

Conclusion

POVERTY HAS ALWAYS BEEN WITH US. DEVELOPMENT ASSISTANCE IS only 50 years old. It is encouraging that there have been huge successes in the aid business—and it is not surprising that there have been some spectacular failures. Many failures involved investments

It is possible to assist development in countries with weak institutions and policies, but the focus needs to be on supporting reformers rather than disbursing money.

based on strategic (not developmental) considerations influenced by the Cold War. But the failures of aid are not simply the result of pursuing nondevelopmental goals. Many of the world's poor live in countries with weak governance and poor policies, so that aid agencies work primarily in difficult environments. Early development thinking suggested that large dollops of capital into these countries would spur development. This is not the case. The examples here show that it is possible to assist development in countries with weak institutions and policies, but the focus needs to be on supporting reformers rather than disbursing money.

A number of common themes run through these examples of effective assistance. There must be *champions of reform with long-term visions* at the local or national level. Aid must help them *create the knowledge that they need for effective development*. In the difficult environments, public services are poor or nonexistent. Since the government in these cases is functioning poorly, effective innovations typically involve *engaging civil society*—either to bring about governmental reform or to create substitute institutions.

While it is possible to make a difference in countries with weak institutions and weak policies, scaling up the assistance to have a large effect generally requires nationwide reform. In Vietnam national reform in the late 1980s set the stage for a dramatic reduction in poverty in the 1990s. But in Cameroon's health sector, a successful innovation in two provinces was not replicated nationally. Essentially, national economic management remained weak and did not take advantage of the successful innovation.

National transformations often catch observers by surprise. No one in the late 1980s could foresee the political and economic transformation that would come over the Soviet Union. Reforms in Vietnam, India in the early 1990s, Ethiopia or El Salvador after their civil wars—all would have been difficult to predict a few years earlier. What this means for donors is that it is worthwhile to look for opportunities to support pockets of reform in difficult cases, but that they will not have much leverage over whether local successes are scaled up to nationwide transformations.

Another common theme concerns donor behavior. In the successful examples of assistance donors were more cooperative than competitive, more focused on knowledge creation than on disbursing money. For donors to be more consistently effective requires changing the internal culture and incentives for line managers in donor agencies—which have often encouraged a focus on the volume of finance or on narrow measures of project "success," not on the contribution of assistance to systemic change. A recent study of aid dependency sponsored by SIDA analyzes the problem:

"Both donor and recipient have incentive systems which reward reaching a high volume of resource transfer, measured in relation to a predefined ceiling.... In many administrations, both bilateral and multilateral, the emphasis is on disbursements and country allocations. Non-disbursed amounts will be noted by executive boards or parliamentary committees and may result in reduced allocations for the next fiscal year.

"On the recipient side, officials of ministries of finance and planning are rewarded for the commitments they can attract from donors in bilateral negotiations or in donor meetings. Whether these commitments result in disbursements is often of less consequence. Results are measured against volume figures, with no regard for the quality of management. Quality is supposed to be measured by regular evaluations, but this dimension of aid transfers is very complex and can always be disputed. Besides, when the time has come to evaluate the actual outcome, most of those responsible for the project on both sides will have been transferred.

"These practices have a direct relationship to program quality as well as to the feeling of program ownership. In the present aid-dependent countries, new programs have been pushed through for decades by donors as well as by planning ministries under a time pressure that appears completely unwarranted in retrospect, considering the slow rate of subsequent implementation. In these often very large-scale programs quality has taken second place behind quantity, and the question of ownership has never arisen: it is the owner who pushes" (Edgren 1996, p. 11).

Effective donor agencies need to create internal mechanisms and incentives that foster selectivity and that focus large-scale finance on developing countries with good policies. In countries with poor policies, donors need to be more patient and accept that the best assistance may involve activities that do not result in much disbursement.

Donor agencies have learned from their successes and failures. In the 1990s all of the major agencies have instituted reforms aimed at strengthening the focus on results on the ground (box 5.1). Most agencies have also formulated country assistance strategies so that individual activities now

Donor agencies need to create internal mechanisms and incentives that foster selectivity and that focus large-scale finance on developing countries with good policies.

Box 5.1 Reforming Aid Agencies in the 1990s

A MAJOR CHALLENGE FOR AID AGENCIES IN RECENT years has been to adapt their institutional strategies, cultures, and capacities to work with participatory development. New patterns of staffing, recruitment, and personnel performance assessment, new project management approaches, and new criteria for judging success—all have emerged progressively. How far has this process gone, and what remains to be done?

For multilateral development banks, self-commissioned reports led to a fundamental reconsideration of the effectiveness of their traditional instruments—project loans. Beginning with the World Bank's Wapenhans Report, followed by similar reports of the Inter-American Development Bank, the Asian Development Bank, and the African Development Bank, the conclusion was that loan quantity had been given primacy over loan quality. Securing loan approvals was a more powerful motivator for staff than working to ensure project success or larger development

goals. Institutional factors critical for sustainable development impact had been neglected. Changes are now under way in each of the multilaterals, and sectorwide approaches are replacing individual projects. The World Bank has embodied its new objectives and organizational culture in a partnership strategy that reaches out to counterparts within and outside government.

Similar changes are evident in bilateral agencies, which have also often been disbursement-driven. But their main instrument has been grants not loans, with more flexibility in preparation and technical assistance. The emphasis has shifted from capital projects to capacity building and support for policy reform.

In all these changes the focus is on development results—on the human progress and the economic, political, and social advance generated by the efforts of the developing countries and their partners.

Source: Development Assistance Committee staff.

---

must fit into a larger game plan for policy reform and institutional change. In the same vein, the focus of evaluation has risen above the level of the project to overall country program reviews. These essentially ask: Have agencies used their resources to stimulate institutional and policy changes that have led to improved services and a better quality of life? This is not an easy question to answer. But it is the right one to ask. The Overseas Development Council recently sponsored reviews of the overall impact of aid in eight African countries, conducted jointly by scholars from the developing countries in question and from major donor countries—which seems to be a fruitful approach. In the same vein, the shareholders of the IMF recently turned to a group of outside scholars to assess the Fund's support to low-income reformers. And the World Bank has initiated country assistance reviews with input from a wide range of stakeholders.

Called for are independent reviews of development agencies with strong input from developing countries and focusing on two questions: Has the bulk of financing gone to sound institutional and policy environments? And have agencies contributed to policy reform and institutional change? Evaluating the right things should feed back into the management and incentives within agencies. With better management and evaluation, development agencies should become:

- *More selective*—putting more money into economies with sound management.
- *More knowledge-based*—using resources to support new approaches to service delivery, expanding knowledge about what works, and disseminating this information as a core business.
- *Better coordinated*—results-oriented agencies should worry less about planting their flags on particular projects and more about how communities, governments, and donors working together can improve services.
- *More self-critical*—agencies continuously should be asking themselves: Why do we do what we do? And what is the impact?

With a better understanding of development and aid effectiveness and with the end of Cold War strategic pressures, there is reason to be optimistic that the reform of aid agencies will succeed.

Appendix 1

Estimating the Effect of Aid on Growth

THE APPENDIXES PROVIDE TECHNICAL DETAILS OF SOME of the important original research results featured in this report. They are based on research papers that are available as journal articles or working papers that can be downloaded from the Assessing Aid website (http://www.worldbank.org/research/aid). The reader who wants more detail should go to these underlying sources. In most cases the datasets will also be available over the web. This first appendix deals with the effect of aid on growth.

The theoretical foundation for recent empirical studies of growth relies on dynamic models of inter-temporal optimization. In these models the accumulation of physical and human capital depends on initial conditions and the institutions and policies that affect the return to savings and investment. Thus, growth is a function of initial conditions, institutions and policies, and external shocks such as changes in the terms of trade or in weather patterns.

To introduce aid, this kind of analysis must take account of the fact that poor growth may induce donors to provide more aid. Instrumental variables techniques essentially split aid flows into permanent and transitory components. Only permanent aid goes into the growth regression. The regressions in table A1.1 use the dataset developed in Burnside and Dollar (1997). The dependent variable is growth rate of per capita GNP, averaged over four-year periods, beginning with 1970–73 and ending with 1990–93. There are six four-year periods and 56 developing countries in the sample (table A1.2), though there are some missing observations where data were not available.

Regression 1 explains growth as a function of initial conditions, the incentive regime, and an error term that captures external shocks. Following other literature, the measures of the incentive regime included are the inflation rate (Fischer 1993), the budget surplus (Easterly and Rebelo 1993), a measure of trade openness (Sachs and Warner 1995), and a measure of institutional quality (Knack and Keefer 1995). The level of government consumption is also considered, but this does not have a robust relationship with growth.

The index of economic management used in this chapter is formed as a weighted sum of the inflation rate, the budget surplus, trade openness, and institutional quality, where the weights are the regression coefficients in regression 1. This index can be interpreted as the predicted growth rate, given the quality of the incentive regime and assuming that the country had the average value of the initial condition variables. The index has a mean of 1.1 with a standard deviation of 1.6. (The phrase "good management" in the text refers to a level of 2.7 or above.)

In regression 2 the index replaces the individual components; it can be seen to have a very strong association with growth. Regression 3 introduces aid relative to GDP and instruments for it with population and variables reflecting donor strategic interests. As in Boone (1994), there is no relationship between aid and growth. The picture changes, however, if aid is interacted with the management index. Regression 4 includes aid interacted with the index, as well as aid squared interacted with the index. (Potential endogeneity requires that instruments be used for aid as well as for both interactive terms.) The positive coefficient on aid times management and the negative coefficient on aid squared times management indicate that aid has a positive effect on growth in a good policy environment but that there are diminishing marginal returns to aid. It should be stressed, however, that the estimate of the diminishing returns is imprecise. To measure this requires cases in which there is good policy and large amounts of aid. There are only a few such cases, so the estimate depends on these few outliers. If they are dropped from the dataset, there is no longer a significant coefficient on the aid squared times management term. However, the positive coefficient on aid times management is quite robust (regression 5).

The sample includes some middle-income countries, such as Chile and Mexico, that have received little aid and have access to international capital markets. Regressions 6–8 repeat regressions 3–5, but drop the middle-income countries. The results are stronger in two senses: first, the estimated impact of aid on growth in a good management environment is larger; and second, the statistical confidence has increased.

For a given quality of policy and level of aid, regressions 4, 5, 7, and 8 each provide a different point estimate of the marginal impact of 1 percent of GDP in aid on growth. The average point estimates for different qualities of policy are:

Marginal effect on growth of 1 percent of GDP in aid (percentage points)

Poor policy (index = 0)	Mediocre policy (1.1)	Good policy (2.7)
–0.3	0	0.5

While the estimated impact of aid in a poor policy environment is negative, the estimate is not statistically different from zero. The estimated impact in a good policy environment is significantly positive. These averages from the four regressions are the estimates shown in Figure 1.5. The positive coefficient on the interactive term also means that policy improvements are more potent if a country is receiving aid. Finally, note that government consumption has no significant relationship with growth—important because aid often finances government consumption (chapter 3).

Table A1.1   Estimating the Effect of Aid on Growth

Dependent variable: growth rate of per capita GNP (four-year average)
Sample: 56 developing countries, four-year periods (1970–73 to 1990–93)

	Regression							
	1	2	3	4	5	6	7	8
Initial GDP per capita	−0.60	−0.63	−0.76	−0.74	−0.95	−0.80	−1.14	−1.42
	(1.04)	(1.30)	(1.00)	(0.90)	(1.09)	(0.82)	(1.22)	(1.27)
Financial depth	0.01	0.01	0.02	0.03	0.02	0.03[a]	0.05[a]	0.03[a]
	(0.95)	(1.12)	(1.68)	(1.66)	(1.62)	(1.99)	(1.99)	(1.99)
Political instability	−0.42	−0.42	−0.39	−0.34	−0.34	−0.72	−0.93	−0.69
	(1.50)	(1.57)	(1.43)	(1.15)	(1.19)	(1.15)	(1.75)	(1.32)
Economic management	—	1.00[b]	1.03[b]	0.50[a]	0.70[b]	1.20[b]	0.01	0.58[a]
		(7.17)	(7.01)	(1.93)	(3.42)	(7.00)	(0.01)	(2.08)
Trade openness	2.11[b]	—	—	—	—	—	—	—
	(4.11)							
Inflation	−1.56[b]	—	—	—	—	—	—	—
	(3.92)							
Budget surplus	4.07	—	—	—	—	—	—	—
	(1.03)							
Institutional quality	0.66[b]	—	—	—	—	—	—	—
	(3.75)							
Government consumption	−2.53	−1.96	−4.38	−1.53	−1.73	−2.38	2.10	1.13
	(0.55)	(0.52)	(0.68)	(0.21)	(0.25)	(0.40)	(0.29)	(0.17)
Aid/GDP	—	—	−0.08	−0.15	−0.37	−0.10	−0.28	−0.53
			(0.28)	(0.35)	(0.89)	(0.49)	(0.79)	(1.69)
Management x aid/GDP	—	—	—	0.66[a]	0.24[a]	—	0.99[b]	0.36[b]
				(2.11)	(2.38)		(2.69)	(3.64)
Management x (aid/GDP)^2	—	—	—	−0.07	—	—	−0.09[a]	—
				(1.63)			(2.10)	
R^2	0.41	0.41	0.39	0.35	0.39	0.46	0.36	0.46
Number of observations	284	284	272	272	268	189	189	185

a. Significant at the 5 percent level.
b. Significant at the 1 percent level.

Table A1.2   Countries in the Dataset

Sub-Saharan Africa	Latin America	Middle East and North Africa	East Asia	South Asia
Botswana	Argentina	Algeria	Indonesia	India
Cameroon	Bolivia	Egypt	Korea	Pakistan
Côte d'Ivoire	Brazil	Morocco	Philippines	Sri Lanka
Ethiopia	Chile	Tunisia	Thailand	
Gabon	Colombia	Syria	Malaysia	
Gambia	Costa Rica	Turkey		
Ghana	Dominican			
Kenya	Republic			
Madagascar	Ecuador			
Malawi	El Salvador			
Mali	Guatemala			
Niger	Guyana			
Nigeria	Haiti			
Senegal	Honduras			
Sierra Leone	Jamaica			
Somalia	Mexico			
Tanzania	Nicaragua			
Togo	Paraguay			
Zaire	Peru			
Zambia	Trinidad			
Zimbabwe	and Tobago			
	Uruguay			
	Venezuela			

Appendix 2

Explaining the Success or Failure of Structural Adjustment Programs

RECENTLY, THE THEORY OF MACROECONOMIC POLICY and economic reforms has changed focus. Instead of viewing the making and implementation of economic policy as a control problem in which the issue is to find the optimal policy rule, the core of the analysis has shifted to the actual policy process. The chosen economic policy is explained by appealing to binding incentive constraints facing optimizing policymakers. The theoretical literature in political economy has identified several factors affecting the likelihood of successful reforms (see Rodrik 1996 for a recent review of the literature). To test these theories, and to investigate if factors under the World Bank's control have any effect on success or failure of reform, a measure of the extent of policy reform is needed.

Previous work on explaining reform progress has used different outcome measures (or changes in them) as proxies of reform, but that has obvious shortcomings. For example, outcome is partly driven by exogenous shocks which are difficult to disentangle from policy effects, there is lag between policy change and outcome, and reforms differ in objectives and may therefore not be captured by a single outcome measure. Dollar and Svensson (1998) avoid these problem by using a zero-one variable reflecting failure or success of reform programs supported by the World Bank (outcome). The binary evaluation variable (outcome) is determined *ex post* by the Operations Evaluation Department (OED) of the World Bank.

Using the zero-one reform measure as dependent variable, a probit regression could be specified relating the probability of successful reform to domestic political economy variables, World Bank effort variables and other controls. The regressions in table A2.1 use the dataset developed in Dollar and Svensson (1998), consisting of 182 completed adjustment loans during the period 1980–95, for which comparable data could be collected: 36 percent of these reform programs were judged not to have met their objectives.

Regression 1 explains the probability of success of reform as a function of only the core political economy variables. All variables enter significantly: success is associated with democratic government and with political stability. Ethnic fractionalization and length of time that the incumbent has been in power enter non-linearly: the basic message is that high degrees of fractionalization are bad for policy reform, and that long-term incumbents are not likely candidates for reform. Regression 1 predicts correctly 75 percent of the observations.

In regression 2, several Bank-related variables are added to the specification, recognizing that there is an endogeneity issue that has not yet been addressed. Some of these variables are likely to be exogenous: whether the adjustment loan focuses on trade reform or sectoral reform depends on the nature of the policy problems in the country and the government's desire to attack particular problems. What is clearly under the Bank's influence is the amount of preparation staffweeks and amount of supervision staffweeks. In regression 2, preparation is positively associated with the probability of success and supervision, negatively associated. Once controlling for these two variables, other Bank-related variables such as number of conditions, loan size and the allocation of conditions among tranches play no role.

An implicit assumption underlying regression 2 is that the World Bank does not respond to exogenous shocks that reduce the probability of success—that is, the error term in regression 2 is assumed to be uncorrelated with the amount of preparation and supervision. However, an exogenous shock that reduces the probability of success is likely to call forth more preparation and supervision resources. Thus, in order to estimate these relationships it is necessary to partition the World Bank effort into a predicted part that is independent of exogenous shocks—and an unpredicted part. This is possible to do by employing a two-stage probit technique developed by Amemiya (1978). Regression 3 reports the result of including the predicted part of the World Bank effort variables. Once these Bank-effort variables are treated as endogenous, there is no relationship between any of them and the success or failure of adjustment programs, while the relationship between the political-economy variables and outcomes is stable. This finding is consistent with the view that there are institutional and political factors that affect the probability of success of a reform program. Given those factors, none of the variables under the World Bank's control significantly affects success or failure of adjustment programs. If endogeneity is ignored, there is a positive relationship between preparation and outcomes, and a negative relationship between supervision and outcomes. That these relationships disappear in the two-stage regressions indicates that the associations reflect how the World Bank allocates resources.

To further explore the last issue, regression equations for supervision and preparation are specified in columns 4-6. Regression 4 shows that preparation is strongly related to a number of variables (regional dummies, loan size, number of conditions, income, and population) that in turn have no relationship with the probability of success—but has very little relationship with the political economy variables.

There is a broadly similar story for the allocation of supervision resources (regressions 5 and 6). Unlike the preparation equation, regional dummies are no longer important. The regional departments of the World Bank have different amounts to prepare loans, but once these loans are approved the regions devote similar resources to supervising a loan of given characteristics. In the supervision equation, it is also considered that preparation may affect supervision. In the OLS regression (regression 5) there is a large, positive relationship between preparation and supervision. This reflects the fact that the error terms in the preparation and supervision equations are certainly correlated. Anything unobserved that leads to higher (lower) than predicted preparation will almost certainly lead to higher (lower) than predicted supervision. The fact that the regional dummies seem to belong in the preparation equation but not in the supervision equation means that it is possible to use them as instruments to correct for this simultaneity problem. In the two-stage least squares regression (regression 6), the relationship between preparation and supervision is no longer significant.

Table A2.1 Estimating the Outcome of Adjustment Loans

	Regression					
	1	2	3	4	5	6
Dependent variable	Outcome	Outcome	Outcome	Preparation	Supervision	Supervision
Regression method	Probit	Probit	Probit/IV[a]	OLS	OLS	IV[a]
Observations	220	182	179	179	179	179
Countries	67	60	60	60	60	60
Constant	−0.098	−0.762	−0.366	3.311	2.685	3.272
	(0.32)	(0.72)	(0.25)	(4.38)	(4.02)	(3.11)
Ethnic fractionalization	5.930	8.176	7.763	0.018	−0.134	−0.144
	(4.16)	(4.40)	(4.04)	(0.04)	(0.42)	(0.46)
Ethnic fractionalization^2	−6.513	−8.501	−8.046	0.043	0.213	0.254
	(4.27)	(4.32)	(3.79)	(0.10)	(0.59)	(0.73)
Government crisis	−1.301	−2.372	−2.285	−0.223	−0.029	−0.017
	(3.94)	(4.46)	(4.29)	(2.48)	(0.39)	(0.18)
Democratically elected	0.585	0.887	0.912	0.124	−6.1E-3	−0.009
	(2.61)	(3.11)	(3.09)	(1.98)	(0.01)	(0.18)
Time in power	−0.089	−0.118	−0.113	0.004	0.003	0.004
	(2.07)	(2.23)	(2.09)	(0.36)	(0.29)	(0.48)
Time in power^2	0.003	0.004	0.004	−3.7E-3	3.6E-3	−4.7E-3
	(2.15)	(2.17)	(2.02)	(0.99)	(1.14)	(1.47)
Preparation staff weeks (log)		0.966	0.323		0.339	0.364
		(2.31)	(0.24)		(5.14)	(1.34)
Supervision staff weeks (log)		−1.410	−0.869			
		(2.92)	(0.67)			
Finance conditions (percent)		1.217	1.423	−0.149	−0.078	−0.120
		(1.84)	(2.02)	(1.07)	(0.67)	(0.99)
Macro and fiscal conditions (percent)		0.910	0.766	−0.260	−0.323	−0.256
		(1.04)	(0.89)	(1.33)	(1.97)	(1.41)
Sectoral conditions (percent)		1.386	1.161	0.002	0.180	0.175
		(2.26)	(1.83)	(0.02)	(1.65)	(1.59)
Trade conditions (percent)		1.067	0.961	−0.021	−0.141	−0.141
		(1.70)	(1.46)	(0.15)	(1.25)	(1.23)
Number of conditions (percent)				0.153	0.074	0.077
				(3.29)	(1.85)	(1.28)
Loan size (log)				0.281	0.210	0.220
				(5.29)	(4.37)	(2.50)
Structural adjustment loan				−0.145	−0.062	−0.105
				(2.16)	(1.10)	(1.58)
Sub-Saharan Africa				−0.080	0.093	
				(0.78)	(1.09)	
Latin America & Caribbean				−0.284	0.020	
				(3.06)	(0.25)	
East Asia				−0.148	−0.118	
				(1.39)	(1.33)	
Initial GDP per capita (log)				−0.064	−0.153	−0.184
				(1.04)	(2.96)	(3.39)
Initial population (log)				−0.147	−0.099	−0.124
				(3.90)	(3.00)	(2.66)
Predicted ability	0.75	0.80				
Adjusted R^2				0.34	0.45	

a. Regression 3 is estimated by a two-stage procedure described in Dollar and Svensson (1998), with preparation and supervision specifications given in regressions 4 and 6. Regression 6 is estimated by 2SLS with preparation specification given in regression 4. t-statistics in parentheses.

Appendix 3

Analysis of the Fungibility of Foreign Aid

ONE OF THE MAIN CHANNELS THROUGH WHICH foreign aid influences development outcomes is its impact on the recipient country's public expenditures. The link between foreign aid and public expenditures is, however, not straightforward because some aid may be "fungible." An aid recipient country could render ear-marked aid fungible by reducing its own resources in the sector that receives aid and transferring them to other sectors of the budget.

Feyzioglu, Swaroop, and Zhu 1998 study this issue using annual data from 1971 to 1990 from 14 countries—Bangladesh, Costa Rica, Ecuador, Egypt, Honduras, Kenya, Mexico, Malawi, Malaysia, Peru, Sierra Leone, Thailand, Turkey, and Zaire. Two foreign aid variables were used: total aid to a country (the annual net disbursement of Official Development Assistance or ODA), and the sectoral composition of concessionary loans from all sources, over time and across countries. Other variables in the data base included total as well as sectoral classification of public spending, per capital real GDP, infant mortality, average years of schooling, school enrollment ratios, military expenditures of neighboring countries, and the share of agriculture in national income.

The model in the study develops links between foreign aid and public spending assuming that the observed mix of public expenditures results from a combination of the government's utility maximizing choice using fungible resources—domestic and external—and the purchase of goods from the nonfungible portion of aid. In the empirical analysis the impact of aggregate foreign aid on total government spending is first estimated to examine whether foreign aid affects the resource mobilization effort of the recipient country. The impact of earmarked sector-specific aid on components of government spending is estimated next and the fungibility hypothesis examined.

While the problem of simultaneity exists in principle in this study, attempt is made to minimize it by (a) using aid disbursement numbers which in most part are predetermined; and (b) including a few economic, political and social indicators of the recipient country as explanatory variables in the regression analysis.

Tables A3.1 and A3.2 report the main regression results of the study. Regression 1 shows a positive and statistically significant relationship between the share of total government expenditure in GDP and the share of the net disbursement of ODA. The regression shows that a dollar increase in foreign aid leads to an increase of 0.95 cents in total government spending. There is no tax relief effect in this sample. Increases in the net disbursement of concessional loans, however, are far more stimulative of total government expenditures. Regression 2 shows that a dollar increase in concessionary loans leads to a $1.24 increase in government expenditures. The likely reason why concessionary loans have a relatively larger impact on government expenditures than overall ODA is that a portion of such loans have matching requirements—that is, for every dollar that a government spends on a specified activity it gets a matching amount in concessionary loans. Among the control variables, the share of agricultural output in GDP—a measure of level of development in a country—is the only variable that is statistically significant in both the equations. The negative coefficient suggests that countries that have a bigger share of their GDP from agriculture and are therefore relatively less developed, have relatively smaller government spending. Regression 3—which includes expenditure shares according to the economic classification—indicates that roughly three-quarters of ODA is spent on government's current expenditure. The coefficient of ODA in regression 5 shows that the remaining one-quarter of aid (after accounting for current expenditure) goes for capital expenditure.

Regressions reported in table A3.2 examine the link between the net disbursement of concessionary loans to a particular sector and public spending in that sector. In each of the six regressions—one each for education, health, energy, agriculture, transport and communication, and defense—the coefficient on the variable *Government expenditure net of aid in GDP*, which is statistically significant in all regressions, indicates how the government distributes an additional dollar that it gets from all resources net of concessionary loans. Regression 5 has a positive and statistically significant relationship between loans to the transport and communication sector and the public spending in that sector; the coefficient on the aid variable is 0.92, which is statistically not different from 1. Other estimates indicate that loans to agriculture and energy, for the sample countries, have been fungible. But for the education and health sectors no null hypotheses of interest can be rejected. The likely explanation is that based on the available data for these sectors, the power of the test is not enough to reject any reasonable hypothesis. In recent years, the donor community has been increasingly concerned that development assistance is being used to fund military expenditures. Data from the sample countries do not, however, support the hypothesis that foreign aid is diverted for military purposes (regression 6). The results show that there is no consistent link between aid to a sector and increased spending in that sector—that is, aid tends to be fungible.

Table A3.1   Impact of Foreign Aid on Total, Current, and Capital Public Expenditures, 1971–90

	Regression					
	Total government spending		Public current expenditures		Public capital expenditures	
Dependent variable[a]	1	2	3	4	5	6
Constant						1.80
						(0.29)
Government expenditure			0.63	0.65	0.35	0.35
net of aid in GDP			(15.33)	(14.44)	(9.15)	(8.80)
Share of ODA in GDP	0.95		0.72		0.29	
	(5.82)		(10.59)		(4.65)	
Share of concessionary		1.24		1.22		0.27
loans in GDP		(4.08)		(8.97)		(1.19)
Real per-capita GDP	0.01	0.01	−0.002	−0.004	0.002	0.002
	(1.67)	(1.10)	(0.43)	(1.05)	(0.59)	(0.80)
Neighbor's military	0.33	0.43	−0.10	−0.53	0.08	0.04
expenditure in GDP [lag(−1)]	(1.04)	(1.26)	(0.76)	(0.37)	(0.64)	(0.30)
Average schooling in	−1.78	−1.12	3.74	2.92	−3.58	−1.95
labor force [lag(−1)]	(1.04)	(0.61)	(4.19)	(2.90)	(4.27)	(2.66)
Infant mortality rate [lag(−1)]	0.09	0.06	0.06	0.01	−0.05	−0.02
	(1.51)	(0.94)	(2.19)	(0.26)	(1.91)	(0.89)
Share of agriculture	−0.63	−0.53	−0.12	−0.09	0.07	0.15
output in GDP [lag(−1)]	(2.69)	(2.09)	(0.94)	(0.63)	(0.59)	(1.55)
Gastil index of political	0.39	0.32	−0.17	−0.48	0.04	−0.03
and civil liberties	(0.64)	(0.50)	(0.50)	(1.35)	(0.12)	(0.10)
Adjusted R^2	*0.87*	*0.84*	*0.97*	*0.97*	*0.79*	*0.19*
Observations	*128*	*128*	*89*	*89*	*89*	*89*
Model[b]	*Fixed*	*Fixed*	*Fixed*	*Fixed*	*Fixed*	*Random*

a. Dependent variables are expressed as a share of gross domestic product (GDP).

b. Model indicates whether the country dummies in the regression represent a fixed effects or a random effects model.

Note: For regressions that represent a fixed-effects model, coefficients of country dummies are not reported. t-statistics in parentheses.

Table A3.2   Impact of Sectoral Concessionary Loans on Sectoral Government Expenditure, 1971–90

Dependent variable[a]	Education 1	Health 2	Energy 3	Agriculture 4	Transport and communication 5	Defense 6
Constant	4.12	1.19	−0.63	−2.07	2.08	3.36
	(1.49)	(1.28)	(0.51)	(1.20)	(3.44)	(0.89)
Government expenditure	0.08	0.02	0.01	0.03	0.10	0.11
Net of aid in GDP	(4.94)	(4.32)	(1.99)	(2.75)	(5.57)	(5.10)
Sectoral loans (as a share of GDP)						
Education	1.55	0.01	0.16	0.05	0.52	0.71
	(1.08)	(0.03)	(0.27)	(0.05)	(0.31)	(0.38)
Health	−3.21	−0.31	3.07	3.45	1.10	5.19
	(0.73)	(0.23)	(1.61)	(1.29)	(0.21)	(0.91)
Energy	−0.71	0.12	0.36	0.21	0.17	0.02
	(1.21)	(1.84)	(3.82)	(1.59)	(3.75)	(0.07)
Agriculture	0.56	0.19	0.09	−0.05	−0.01	0.21
	(2.22)	(2.45)	(0.82)	(0.32)	(0.03)	(0.65)
Transport and communication	−0.59	0.14	0.16	0.21	0.92	0.36
	(3.01)	(2.44)	(1.92)	(1.77)	(3.98)	(1.44)
Other sectors	−0.05	0.02	0.01	0.06	0.04	−0.01
	(1.65)	(2.30)	(0.79)	(3.25)	(1.09)	(0.35)
Real per capita GDP	0.0003	−0.0001	0.001	0.0003	−0.0002	0.0002
	(0.26)	(0.15)	(1.44)	(0.45)	(0.17)	(0.15)
Neighbor's military expenditure in GDP [lag (−1)]	−0.12	0.003	0.02	−0.004	−0.04	0.01
	(1.28)	(0.17)	(0.41)	(0.12)	(0.67)	(0.16)
Average schooling in labor force [lag (−1)]	−0.19	−0.08	−0.12	0.46	−1.65	−0.29
	(0.68)	(0.89)	(0.99)	(2.55)	(4.87)	(0.75)
Infant mortality rate [lag (−1)]	0.01	−0.003	0.002	0.01	−0.03	−0.01
	(1.37)	(0.91)	(0.53)	(1.60)	(2.38)	(1.12)
Share of agriculture output in GDP [lag (−1)]	−0.05	0.008	0.02	−0.004	−0.08	−0.03
	(1.17)	(0.65)	(1.12)	(0.18)	(1.92)	(0.56)
Gastil index of political and civil liberties	−0.17	−0.06	−0.06	−0.02	−0.07	−0.03
	(1.56)	(1.92)	(1.23)	(0.32)	(0.57)	(0.2)
Adjusted R^2	*0.04*	*0.24*	*0.18*	*0.09*	*0.89*	*0.34*
Observations	*128*	*128*	*128*	*128*	*128*	*128*
Model[b]	*Random*	*Random*	*Random*	*Random*	*Random*	*Random*

See Table 1.

a. Dependent variables are expressed as a share of gross domestic product (GDP).

b. Model indicates whether the country dummies in the regression represent a fixed effects or a random effects model.

Note: For regressions that represent a fixed-effects model, coefficients of country dummies are not reported. t-statistics in parentheses.

Appendix 4

The Impact of Civil Liberties and Democracy on Government Performance

TO MEASURE "CIVIL LIBERTIES" THE STUDY UNDERTAKEN as part of the research on aid effectiveness used a variety of existing indicators constructed by political scientists (Isham, Kaufmann, and Pritchett 1997). The two most general indicators were the Freedom House (1997) civil liberties index which ranks countries annually on a seven-point scale based on assessments of 14 factors, such as a press free of censorship, freedom of assembly and demonstration, freedom of religion, and free trade unions. A different index compiled by Humana (1996) ranks countries on a scale from 0 to 100 on the degree to which the country complies with the human rights agreed to in the 1966 UN Covenant on Civil and Political Rights.

To measure "democracy," there are similar rankings constructed by political scientists that focus more narrowly on the extent to which a country's leaders (executive and legislative) were chosen by elections. This includes a political index of democracy created by Freedom House (1997) as well as others.

To measure the performance of governments we used a sample of the economic rates of return (ERR) of World Bank projects, which requires some explanation. Since the World Bank applies the same project selection and implementation procedures across all countries, the *differences* across countries in returns are an indication of how effective the government is in implementing public projects.

To assess the impact of the governance variables we began from a base specification of the determinants of ERR from Isham and Kaufmann (forthcoming), which included a set of policy variables (black market premia, fiscal surplus), economic variables (terms of trade changes, GDP growth, the capital to labor ratio), a dummy for "project complexity" and a set of dummy variables for the sector of the project. For the time-varying variables, we used the average value in the three years prior to the year in which the project was evaluated (usually the same as the completion year). We experimented with and without a set of regional dummy variables. Table A4.1 shows the base case results, estimated using a Tobit procedure to allow for the downward truncation of the dependent variable (the ERR is truncated as –5).

To this equation are added the variables for civil liberties. Both civil liberties variables had a strong positive and statistically significant impact on the performance of Bank-financed government projects (table A4.2). The two variables produce qualitatively similar results and the range of the estimates suggests that improving from the worst to the best civil liberties would improve the rate of return on government investment projects by between 8 percentage points (Freedom House index) and 22 (Humana index) (the average return in the sample was 16).

Two other interesting results from this regression suggest that this impact reflected the impact of citizen voice on the performance of government. First, indicators of civil strife (riots, political strikes and demonstrations) are *positively* related to the ERR on Bank projects, but that partial correlation is explained by the fact that there is more of this expression of discontent in countries with *more* civil liberties. Once one accounts for the greater civil liberties, this eliminates any independent impact of civil strife, indicating that when civil liberties allow it there is greater expression of all types of citizen voice and that ultimately this voice is a force for improving government performance.

Second, once the regressions explaining project returns included civil liberties there was no additional impact of electoral democracy. So, while electoral democracy and civil liberties are obviously closely linked, both in practice and in the data, the main channel of influence appears to be the availability of civil liberties rather than the more purely political mechanisms of choosing leaders.

Table A4.1 Base Specification for the Nongovernance Determinants of the Economic Rate of Return of Government Projects, 1974–87

	Estimate without regional dummies	Estimate with regional dummies
Exogenous variable		
In (capital/labor)	−1.09	−1.66
	(0.067)[a]	(0.060)[a]
Dummy for project complexity	−4.29	−4.23
	(0.017)[b]	(0.016)[b]
Terms of trade shock	0.0015	0.001
	(0.889)	(0.922)
Policy variable		
Black market premia	−0.046	−0.037
	(0.000)[b]	(0.000)[b]
Fiscal surplus	0.197	0.266
	(0.149)	(0.063)[a]
GDP growth	0.193	0.013
	(0.357)	(0.949)
Regional dummy variable		
East Asia		−3.33
		(0.154)
Latin American and the Caribbean		−4.74
		(0.072)[a]
Europe, the Middle East, and North Africa		−4.93
		(0.100)[a]
Sub-Saharan Africa		−10.8
		(0.000)[b]
Sectoral dummy variable		
Agriculture	0.027	1.39
	(0.992)	(0.602)
Energy and public utilities	−3.92	−3.18
	(0.136)	(0.220)
Transport and tourism	3.85	6.24
	(0.137)	(0.016)[b]
Urban	10.1	11.9
	(0.011)[b]	(0.003)[b]

a. p-level less than 0.10.

b. p-level less than 0.05.

Note: We report p-levels of the test whether the coefficient is 0 rather than test statistics themselves. The p-level is the significance level at which the null hypothesis can be rejected, hence a p-level less than 0.05 indicates a rejection of the null hypothesis at (at least) the 5 percent level. The p-levels are in parentheses. The sample size is 761.

Table A4.2 Impact of Civil Liberties Indicators on the Economic Rate of Return of Government Projects, Controlling for Economic and Project Variables

Index	Without regional variables	With regional variables
Freedom House civil liberties, 1978–87	1.95 (0.000)[a]	1.32 (0.047)[a]
Humana, 1982–85	0.251 (0.009)[a]	0.256 (0.025)[a]

a. p-level less than 0.05.

Note: Sample sizes are 649 for the Freedom House civil liberties index and 236 for the Humana index.

Appendix 5
Estimating the Impact of Analytical Work

W
HILE THERE HAVE BEEN VARIOUS ANALYSES OF
the impact of aid in the aggregate, far less
attention has been devoted to investigating
the impact of different types of aid and the
composition of the aid portfolio. Of particular importance in this context is the relationship between financial transfers and analytical work. This
distinction, and the effort to measure the impact and economic return
to analytical services, is of particular relevance in a context where, with
increasing access of developing countries to nonconcessional sources of
finance, it is often argued that the comparative advantage of international
institutions such as the World Bank will shift toward the provision of
such "non-lending" services.

In the case of the World Bank, such analytical work comprises two
distinct areas. Countrywide studies include Economic Memoranda con-
taining a comprehensive account of economic performance and
prospects, as well as topical reports such as Poverty Assessments, Public
Expenditure Reviews, and so on that underpin the World Bank's policy
advice. These are complemented by sectoral studies such as reviews of
the Transport Sector, Health and Education Sector Reports—which provide the broad framework that generally serves as a basis for subsequent
lending operations in these sectors. Undertaking this range and magnitude of work does not come cheap—annual expenditures on economic
analysis and advice are more than $100 million.

Issues, Approach, and Data

The three key questions addressed in Deininger, Squire, and Basu (1998) are (1) whether economic and sector work (ESW) enhances project quality, thereby making a positive contribution to development impact; (2) whether reallocation of staff time from activities related to supervision or preparation of specific projects to ESW or vice versa could have enhanced overall project quality; and (3) whether other goals, such as a tradeoff between lending volume and lending quality, might have guided the allocation of scarce staff resources. Estimation of reduced form equations for project quality (as well as demand for resources in preparation and supervision of projects, respectively) that can be derived from the manager's assumed objective function provides a basis for empirical testing of these hypotheses. Information on project performance is based on ratings of the Bank's Operations Evaluation Department (OED) of either the rate of return as estimated after project completion (for the set of projects where such an estimation is actually feasible) or a zero-one rating that classifies a project as either satisfactory or unsatisfactory. These measures are available for 1,367 and 3,957 projects, respectively, although availability of data on ESW inputs somewhat reduces the sample.

Results

This approach finds that ESW has a significant positive impact on various measures of quality of World Bank projects. As table A5.1 indicates, a one-staffweek increase in the amount of time devoted to ESW before project initiation is associated with an increase in the economic rate of return for an individual project of between 0.02 and 0.04 percentage points, translating into an increase of between $12,000 and $25,000 in the project's net present value for an all-inclusive cost (with overheads, travel, and so on) of no more than $3,000—a dollar of ESW yields four to eight dollars in development impact. To the extent that a staffweek of ESW benefits more than one project, this would be an underestimate. Indeed, examining the impact of ESW on a country's entire lending program indicates that a dollar of ESW yields between 12 and 15 dollars of development impact. And even this figure fails to capture nonproject related benefits of ESW—as in influencing broader policy formulation and analysis in specific countries.

A question that arises from the analysis is whether the allocation of resources between different types of support has been appropriate. Assuming that staff resources are fungible across time and between different uses, one would expect the marginal contribution of ESW to the quality of lending to be lower than that of lending services (preparation and supervision), because—in contrast to lending services—ESW can have benefits beyond its immediate impact on lending. Indeed, ESW is often undertaken to provide the basis for policy advice to governments and is not necessarily tightly linked to a particular project or lending program. Deininger, Squire, and Basu find the reverse, however—ESW has a systematically positive effect on the quality of the lending program, whereas neither preparation nor supervision turn out to be significant. This suggests that reallocation of staff time from lending services to ESW would have increased the quality of the lending program. Consistent with this, we find that task managers at the project level are able to reduce the time allocated to lending services by about 2.5 staffweeks for every staffweek expended on ESW. We infer that ESW helps staff to identify and support new investment options (it expands the set of feasible projects) and design better projects *ex ante* (it improves the quality of projects already in the investment program). Preparation

Table A5.1   Impact of Economic and Sector Work on Project Outcome and Economic Rate of Return

Dependent Variable	Project Outcome	Rate of Return
ESW	0.090[b]	4.229[c]
	(0.407)	(1.664)
Public sector surplus	0.719	14.974
	(0.963)	(53.654)
Inflation	−0.037[a]	1.917
	(.021)	(10.248)
Openness	0.739[c]	−3.495
	(0.018)	(21.888)
No of projects	*873*	*302*
R^2/LL	*−534.62*	*0.142*

a. Significant at the 10 percent level.
b. Significant at the 5 percent level.
c. Significant at the 1 percent level.
Note: Coefficients and standard error multiplied by 100. Sector dummies included but not reported. Standard errors in parentheses.

and supervision, by contrast, can improve the quality of a project (whether good or bad) only *ex post*.

Even though the preceding results suggest that higher levels of ESW will improve the quality of the lending program, it is still possible that, within a given resource envelope, shifting staff time from lending services to ESW will reduce the overall lending volume. Addressing this question, we find that this was indeed the case—lending services were between 40 and 50 percent more effective in increasing total commitments than ESW. But if disbursements—resource transfer—is the variable of interest, we find that managers could have increased both lending quality and disbursements by switching resources from lending services to ESW. This, together with the conclusion that there has been underinvestment in ESW from the standpoint of project quality, suggests that the volume of commitments has (at least to some degree) been an additional objective guiding the disposition of staff resources. These results provide some insight into this tradeoff between quality and quantity— the analysis suggests that on average a manager was indifferent between a decrease of $2 million in the net present value of a lending program and an additional $4 million of lending volume. If this estimate is broadly accurate, it suggests that managers were prepared to allow a substantial reduction in program quality in return for only a small increase (2 percent) in commitments relative to the average program size.

Selected Bibliography

Alesina, Alberto, and David Dollar, 1998, "Who Gives Aid to Whom and Why?" NBER Working Paper 6612. National Bureau of Economic Research, Cambridge, Mass.

Amemiya, T. 1978. "The Estimation of a Simultaneous Equation Generalized Probit Model." *Econometrica* 46.

Bauer, P.T. 1971. *Dissent on Development.* London: Weidenfeld and Nicolson.

Berg, Elliott. 1993. *Rethinking Technical Cooperation: Reforms for Capacity Building in Africa.* New York: United Nations Development Programme.

Birdsall, Nancy, and François Orivel. 1996. "Demand for Primary Schooling in Rural Mali: Should User Fees Be Increased?" *Education Economics* 4(3).

Boone, Peter. 1994. "The Impact of Foreign Aid on Savings and Growth." London School of Economics.

Branson, William, and Carl Jayarajah. 1995. *Structural and Sectoral Adjustment: World Bank Experience, 1980–92.* A World Bank Operations Evaluation Study. Washington, D.C.

Bruno, Michael, Martin Ravallion, and Lyn Squire. 1998. "Equity and Growth in Developing Countries: Old and New Perspectives on the Policy Issues." In V. Tanzi and K. Chu, eds., *Income Distribution and High-Quality Growth.* Cambridge, Mass.: MIT Press.

Burnside, Craig, and David Dollar. 1997. "Aid, Policies, and Growth." Policy Research Working Paper 1777. World Bank, Development Research Group, Washington, D.C.

———. 1998. "Aid, the Incentive Regime, and Poverty Reduction." Policy Research Working Paper 1937. World Bank, Development Research Group, Washington, D.C.

Campos, Ed, and Sanjay Pradhan. 1996. "Budgetary Institutions and Expenditure Outcomes: Binding Government to Fiscal Performance." Policy Research Working Paper 1646. World Bank, Policy Research Department, Washington, D.C.

Carapetis, Steve, Hernán Levy, and Terje Wolden. 1991. *The Road Maintenance Initiative: Building Capacity for Policy Reform.* EDI Seminar Series. Washington, D.C.: World Bank.

Cashel-Cordo, P., and S. Craig. 1990. "The Public Sector Impact of International Resource Transfers." *Journal of Development Economics* 32(3).

Cassen, Robert. 1994. *Does Aid Work?* Oxford: Clarendon.

Chang, Charles, Eduardo Fernandez-Arias, and Luís Serven. 1998. "Measuring Aid Flows: A New Approach." World Bank, Development Research Group, Washington, D.C.

Collier, Paul. 1997. "The Failure of Conditionality." In C. Gwin and J. Nelson, eds., *Perspectives on Aid and Development.* Washington, D.C.: Overseas Development Council.

Collier, Paul, and David Dollar. 1998. "Aid Allocation and Poverty Reduction." World Bank, Development Research Group, Washington, D.C.

Deininger, Klaus, Lyn Squire, and Swati Basu. 1998. "Does Economic Analysis Improve the Quality of Foreign Assistance?" *World Bank Economic Review* 12(3).

Devarajan, Shantayanan, Vinaya Swaroop, and Heng-fu Zou. 1996. "The Composition of Public Expenditure and Economic Growth." *Journal of Monetary Economics* 37.

Dollar, David, and William Easterly. 1998. "The Search for the Key: Aid, Investment, and Policies in Africa." World Bank, Development Research Group, Washington, D.C.

Dollar, David, Jennie Litvack, and Paul Glewwe, eds.1998. *Household Welfare and Vietnam's Transition.* Washington, D.C.: World Bank.

Dollar, David, and Jakob Svensson. 1998. "What Explains the Success or Failure of Structural Adjustment Programs?" Policy Research Working Paper 1938. World Bank, Development Research Group, Washington, D.C.

Easterly, William. 1997. "The Ghost of Financing Gap." Policy Research Working Paper 1807. World Bank, Development Research Group, Washington, D.C.

Easterly, William, Michael Kremer, Lant Pritchett, and Lawrence Summers. 1993. "Good Policy or Good Luck? Country Growth Performance and Temporary Shocks." *Journal of Monetary Economics* 32(3).

Easterly, William, and Sergio T. Rebelo. 1993. "Fiscal Policy and Economic Growth: An Empirical Investigation." *Journal of Monetary Economics* 32(3).

Edgren, Gus. 1996. "A Challenge to the Aid Relationship." In SIDA (1996).

Ehrenpreis, Dag. 1997. "The Changing Global Framework." In SIDA (1997a).

El Salvador, Ministry of Education. 1995. *EDUCO Learns and Teaches.* San Salvador: Algier's Impresores, SA de CV.

Fallon, Peter R., and Luiz Pereira da Silva. 1995. "Recognizing Labor Market Constraints: Government -Donor Competition for Manpower in Mozambique." In Lindauer and Nunberg (1995).

Feyzioglu, Tarhan, Vinaya Swaroop, and Min Zhu. 1998. "A Panel Data Analysis of the Fungibility of Foreign Aid." *World Bank Economic Review* 12(1).

Filmer, Deon, Jeffrey Hammer, and Lant Pritchett. 1998. "Health Policy in Poor Countries: Weak Links in the Chain." Policy Research Working Paper 1874. World Bank, Development Research Group, Washington, D.C.

Filmer, Deon, and Lant Pritchett. 1997. "Child Mortality and Public Spending on Health: How Much Does Money Matter?" Policy Research Working Paper 1864. World Bank, Development Research Group, Washington, D.C.

Fischer, Stanley. 1993. "The Role of Macroeconomic Factors in Growth." *Journal of Monetary Economics* 32(3).

Fraker, Thomas, Alberto Martini, and James Ohls. 1995. "The Effect of Food Stamp Cashout on Food Expenditures: An Assessment of the Findings from Four Demonstrations." *Journal of Human Resources* 30(4).

Freedom House. 1997. *Freedom in the World: Political Rights and Civil Liberties.* New York.

Haltiwanger, John, and Manisha Singh. Forthcoming. "Cross-Country Evidence on Public Sector Retrenchment." *World Bank Economic Review.*

Hanushek, Eric, and Dongwook Kim. 1995. "Schooling, Labor Force Quality, and Economic Growth." NBER Working Paper 5399. National Bureau of Economic Research, Cambridge, Mass.

Heggie, Ian. 1994. *Management and Financing of Roads: An Agenda for Reform.* World Bank Technical Paper 275. Washington, D.C.

Hilton, Rita. 1990. "Cost Recovery and Local Resource Mobilization: An Examination of Incentives in Irrigation Systems in Nepal." Burlington, Vt.: Associates in Rural Development.

———. 1992. "Institutional Incentives for Resource Mobilization: An Analysis of Irrigation Schemes in Nepal." *Journal of Theoretical Politics* 4(3).

Hirschman, A. 1967. *Development Projects Observed.* Twentieth Century Fund. New York.

Hulten, Charles R. 1996. "Infrastructure Capital and Economic Growth: How Well You Use It May Be More Important than How Much You Have." NBER Working Paper 5847. National Bureau of Economic Research, Cambridge, Mass.

Humana, Charles. 1996. *World Human Rights Guide.* London: Hodder and Stroughton.

Isham, Jonathan, and Daniel Kaufmann. Forthcoming. "The Forgotten Rationale for Policy Reform: The Impact on Projects." *Quarterly Journal of Economics.*

Isham, Jonathan, Daniel Kaufmann, and Lant Pritchett. 1997. "Civil Liberties, Democracy, and the Performance of Government Projects." *World Bank Economic Review* 11(2).

Isham, Jonathan, Deepa Narayan, and Lant Pritchett. 1995. "Does Participation Improve Performance? Establishing Causality with Subjective Data." *World Bank Economic Review* 9(2).

Ishikawa, Shigeru. 1960. *Economic Development in Asian Perspective.* Tokyo: Kinokuniya.

———. 1978. *Labor Absorption in Asian Agriculture.* Bangkok: ILO-ARTEP.

Jha, Shikha, and Vinaya Swaroop. 1997. "Fiscal Effects of Foreign Aid: A Case Study of India." World Bank, Development Research Group, Washington, D.C.

Jimenez, Emmanuel, and Yasuyuki Sawada. 1998. "Do Community-Managed Schools Work? An Evaluation of El Salvador's EDUCO Program." Impact Evaluation of Education Reforms Working Paper 8. World Bank, Development Research Group, Washington, D.C.

Jones, William. 1995. *The World Bank and Irrigation.* A World Bank Operations Evaluation Study. Washington, D.C.

Killick, Tony. 1991. "The Developmental Effectiveness of Aid to Africa." Policy Research Working Paper 646. World Bank, International Economics Department, Washington, D.C.

Kim, Jooseop, Harold Alderman, and Peter Orazem. 1998. "Can Private Schools Subsidies Increase Schooling for the Poor? The Quetta Urban Fellowship Program." Impact Evaluation of Education Reforms Working Paper 11. World Bank, Development Research Group, Washington, D.C.

Knack, Stephen, and Philip Keefer. 1995. "Institutions and Economic Performance: Cross-Country Tests Using Alternative Institutional Measures." *Economics and Politics* 7(3).

Krueger, Anne O., Constantine Michalopoulos, and Vernon Ruttan. 1989. *Aid and Development.* Baltimore and London: Johns Hopkins University Press.

Levy, Victor. 1987. "Does Concessionary Aid Lead to Higher Investment Rates in Low-Income Countries?" *Review of Economics and Statistics.* 69(1)

Li, Hongyi, Lyn Squire, and Heng-fu Zou. 1998. "Explaining International and Intertemporal Variations in Income Inequality." *Economic Journal* 108.

Lindauer, David, and Barbara Nunberg, eds. 1995. *Rehabilitating Government: Pay and Employment Reform in Africa.* Washington, D.C.: World Bank.

Lindert, Peter. 1994. "The Rise of Social Spending, 1880–1930." *Explorations in Economic History* 31(1).

Little, I.M.D., and J.M. Clifford. 1965. *International Aid.* London: George Allen and Unwin.

Litvack, Jennie, and Claude Bodart. 1993. "User Fees Plus Quality Equals Improved Access to Health Care: Results of a Field Experiment in Cameroon." *Social Science and Medicine* 37(3).

Ljunggren, Borje. 1993. "Market Economies under Communist Regimes: Reform in Vietnam, Laos and Cambodia." In B. Ljunggren, ed., *The Challenge of Reform in Indochina.* Cambridge, Mass.: Harvard University Press.

Lopez, Cecilia. 1997. *Impacto de la Ayuda Externa en America Latina, 1972–1992* (Impact of External Aid on Latin America, 1972–1992). Bogotá: Tercer Mundo.

Lucas, Robert. 1988. "On the Mechanics of Economic Development." *Journal of Monetary Economics* 22(1).

Marshall, Katherine. 1997. "Vision and Relationships in the International Aid World: The Gambia–World Bank Kairaba Partnership Forum." HIID Discussion Paper 602. Harvard Institute for International Development, Cambridge, Mass.

Mauro, Paul. 1995. "Corruption and Growth." *Quarterly Journal of Economics* 110.

McCarthy, Desmond. 1995. "Review of Public Expenditure Work." World Bank, Policy Research Department, Washington, D.C.

Moffitt, Robert. 1989. "Estimating the Value of an In-Kind Transfer: The Case of Food Stamps." *Econometrica* 57(2).

Mosley, Paul. 1987a. "Conditionality as a Bargaining Process: Structural Adjustment Lending, 1980–86." Princeton Essays in International Finance 168. Princeton University, Princeton, N.J.

———. 1987b. *Overseas Aid: Its Defence and Reform.* Brighton, England: Wheatsheaf.

Mosley, Paul, Jane Harrigan, and John Toye. 1995. *Aid and Power.* Vol. 1. 2d ed. London: Routledge.

Musgrove, Philip. 1996. *Public and Private Roles in Health: Theory and Financing Patterns.* World Bank Discussion Paper 339. Washington, D.C.

Narayan, Deepa. 1995. *The Contribution of People's Participation: Evidence from 121 Rural Water Supply Projects.* Environmentally Sustainable Development Occasional Paper 1. Washington, D.C.: World Bank.

North, Douglass. 1990. *Institutions, Institutional Change and Economic Performance.* Cambridge: Cambridge University Press.

OECD (Organisation for Economic Co-operation and Development). 1998. *Development Cooperation: 1997 Report.* Paris.

———. 1996. *Shaping the 21st Century: The Role of Development Cooperation.* Paris.

———. 1992. *Principles for Effective Aid.* Paris.

OECF (Overseas Economic Cooperation Fund) of Japan. 1996. *The Role of OECF toward 2010.* Tokyo.

OECF of Japan and World Bank. 1998. *A New Vision of Development Cooperation for the 21st Century.* Proceedings of a symposium held in Tokyo, September 1997. Tokyo

Ostrom, Elinor. 1996. "Incentives, Rules of the Game, and Development." In Michael Bruno and Boris Pleskovic, eds., *Annual World Bank Conference on Development Economics 1995.* Washington, D.C.: World Bank.

Pack, Howard, and Janet Rothenberg Pack. 1990, "Is Foreign Aid Fungible? The Case of Indonesia." *Economic Journal* 100(March).

———. 1993. "Foreign Aid and the Question of Fungibility." *Review of Economics and Statistics* 75(2).

———. 1996. "Foreign Aid and Fiscal Stress." University of Pennsylvania, Philadelphia.

Pritchett, Lant. 1996. "Mind Your P's and Q's: The Cost of Public Investment Is Not the Value of Public Capital." Policy Research Working Paper 1660. World Bank, Development Research Group, Washington, D.C.

———. 1998. "Patterns of Economic Growth: Hills, Plateaus, Mountains, and Plains." Policy Research Working Paper 1947. World Bank, Development Research Group, Washington, D.C.

Ranis, Gustav. 1995. "On Fast-Disbursing Policy-Based Loans." Yale University, Economics Department, New Haven.

Ravallion, Martin, and Shaohua Chen. 1997. "What Can New Survey Data Tell Us about Recent Changes in Distribution and Poverty?" *World Bank Economic Review* 11(2).

Riddell, Roger. 1996. *Aid in the 21st Century.* ODS Discussion Paper Series. United Nations Development Programme, Office of Development Studies. New York: United Nations.

Riddell, R.C., A. Bebbington, and L. Peck. 1995. *Promoting Development by Proxy: An Evaluation of the Development Impact of Government Support to Swedish NGOs.* SIDA Evaluation Report 1995/2. Stockholm: Swedish International Development Authority.

Rodrik, Dani. 1996. "Understanding Economic Policy Reform." *Journal of Economic Literature* 34(1).

Sachs, Jeffrey. 1994. "Life in the Economic Emergency Room." In Williamson (1994).

Sachs, Jeffrey, and Andrew Warner. 1995. "Economic Reform and the Process of Global Integration." *Brookings Papers on Economic Activity,* no. 1.

SIDA (Swedish International Development Authority). 1996. *Aid Dependency.* Stockholm.

———. 1997a. *Development Cooperation in the 21st Century.* Stockholm.

———. 1997b. *SIDA Looks Forward.* Stockholm.

Summers, Robert, and Alan Heston. 1991. "The Penn World Table, Version V." *Quarterly Journal of Economics* 106.

Swaroop, Vinaya. 1997. "Experience with Public Expenditure Reviews." World Bank, Development Research Group, Washington, D.C.

Tan, Jee-Peng, and Alain Mingat. 1992. *Education in Asia: A Comparative Study of Cost and Financing.* A World Bank Regional and Sectoral Study. Washington, D.C.

Tendler, Judith. 1975. *Inside Foreign Aid.* Baltimore: Johns Hopkins University Press.

Thomas, Vinod, Ajay Chhibber, Mansour Dailami, and Jaime de Melo, eds. 1991. *Restructuring Economies in Distress: Policy Reform and the World Bank.* New York: Oxford University Press.

Thompson, Louis S., and Karim-Jacques Budin. 1997. "Global Trend to Railway Concessions Delivering Positive Results." Viewpoint 134. World Bank, Finance, Private Sector, and Infrastructure Network, Washington, D.C.

United Kingdom, Secretary of State for International Development. 1997. *Eliminating World Poverty: A Challenge for the 21st Century.* White Paper on International Development. London.

van de Walle, Dominique. 1995. "The Distribution of Subsidies through Public Health Services in

Indonesia, 1978–87." In Dominique van de Walle and Kimberly Nead, eds., *Public Spending and the Poor.* Baltimore: Johns Hopkins University Press.

van de Walle, Nicholas, and Timothy Johnston. 1996. *Improving Aid to Africa.* Washington, D.C.: Overseas Development Council.

Wade, Robert. 1995. "The Ecological Basis of Irrigation Institutions: East and South Asia." *World Development* 23.

White, H. 1992. "The Macroeconomic Analysis of Aid Impact." *Journal of Development Studies* 28.

Williamson, John, ed. 1994. *The Political Economy of Policy Reform.* Washington, D.C.: Institute for International Economics.

World Bank. 1992. "Effective Implementation: Key to Development Impact." Report of the World Bank's Management Task Force. Washington, D.C.

———. 1993. *World Development Report 1993: Investing in Health.* New York: Oxford University Press.

———. 1994. *World Development Report 1994: Infrastructure for Development.* New York: Oxford University Press.

———. 1995. *World Development Report 1995: Workers in an Integrating World.* New York: Oxford University Press.

———. 1996a. "Resettlement and Development: The Bankwide Review of Projects Involving Involuntary Resettlement, 1986–1993." Environment Department Paper 032. Washington, D.C.

———. 1996b. "Technical Assistance." Lessons and Practices 7. World Bank, Operations Evaluation Department, Washington, D.C.

———. 1997a. "Annual Review of Development Effectiveness." Report 17196. World Bank, Operations Evalution Department, Washington, D.C.

———. 1997b. *World Development Report 1997: The State in a Changing World.* New York: Oxford University Press.

———. 1998a. *Global Development Finance 1998.* Washington, D.C.

———. 1998b. *World Development Indicators 1998.* Washington, D.C.